W9-DJI-248

Foundations of Modern Sociology Series

Alex Inkeles, *Editor*

Foundations of Modern Sociology Series

the family

William J. Goode, *Columbia University*

Prentice-Hall, Inc., *Englewood Cliffs, New Jersey*

Prentice-Hall Foundations of Modern Sociology Series

Alex Inkeles, *Editor*

© *Copyright 1964 by PRENTICE-HALL, INC., Englewood Cliffs, New Jersey.*
All rights reserved. No part of this book may be reproduced
in any form, by mimeograph or any other means, without permission
in writing from the publisher. Printed in the United States of America.
Library of Congress Catalog No.: 64–17074.
Designed by Harry Rinehart

Current printing (last digit):

13   12

PRENTICE-HALL INTERNATIONAL, INC., *London*
PRENTICE-HALL OF AUSTRALIA, PTY., LTD., *Sydney*
PRENTICE-HALL OF CANADA, LTD., *Toronto*
PRENTICE-HALL OF INDIA PRIVATE LIMITED, *New Delhi*
PRENTICE-HALL OF JAPAN, INC., *Tokyo*

C–30181(*p*), C–30182(*c*)

preface

In these pages, I have tried to exemplify, rather than argue, the fruitfulness of sociological theory when applied to family relations. Hopefully, the serious reader will see not only the framework of ideas that here encompasses a wide range of facts, but also will realize how using such a framework will elucidate still other observations not here reported. This text also utilizes data from other societies, both present and past, to extend our range of experience, to qualify our generalizations, to test our hypotheses, and to show in general that twentieth-century sociology can no longer be bound by a parochialism that confines its vision to the urban centers of the contemporary United States. In so doing, the book suggests that a well-trained young sociologist with a historical bent will find much work to do, since we have few reliable studies on family systems of the past.

In pointing to the complex relations between family systems and the larger social structure, I am arguing implicitly that the family can no longer be treated as a simple set of dependent variables explained by cryptic remarks about "economic forces." The aim of a social theorist is to state and demonstrate determinate relationships between sets of central variables, no matter which may turn out to be "dependent." In any event, a systematic attempt to explain *any* important institution is likely to force the researcher to explore the larger social structure. Thus, I am urging the wise student of society to give serious thought to the importance of the family system.

Finally, a word with respect to the general problem of values. It is sometimes useful to remember that science focuses on what is, how people actually behave and feel, and that science cannot tell us how we ought to behave. It is therefore almost unnecessary to state that my analyses of particular family patterns do not imply approval of them. But I mean more. I think that sociology as a science can justifiably explore from time to time some alternative modes of living; can suggest possible utopias. This is not, however, a task of salon sociology. We should be well equipped with sound theory and facts before posing such solutions. Whether or not we work out better family systems, at least some of our future social planning will be wiser if we base it on the best of sound sociological research; and sociological wisdom will increasingly have to take systematic account of family patterns.

William J. Goode

contents

the family
as an element
in the
social structure

one

In all known societies, almost everyone lives his life enmeshed in a network of family rights and obligations called role relations. A person is made aware of his role relations through a long period of socialization during his childhood, a process in which he learns how others in his family expect him to behave, and in which he himself comes to feel this is both the right and the desirable way to act. Some, however, find their obligations a burden, or do not care to take advantage of their rights. This wide range of behavior leads to one of the commonest themes of conversation found in all societies—just what the duties of a given child or parent, husband or wife, cousin or uncle ought to be, and then, whether he *has done* his duty. This type of discussion is especially common in societies undergoing industrialization, where arguments are frequent concerning the duties of women.

Various Views of the Family

The intense emotional meaning of family relations for almost all members of a society has been observable throughout man's history. Philosophers and social analysts have noted that society is a structure made up of *families*, and that the peculiarities of a given society can be described by outlining its family relations. The earliest moral and ethical writings suggest

1

that a society loses its strength if people fail in their family obligations. Confucius thought, for example, that happiness and prosperity would prevail in the society if only everyone would behave "correctly" as a family member—which primarily meant that no one should fail in his filial obligations. The relationship between a ruler and his subjects, then, was parallel to that of a father and his children. Similarly, much of the early Hebrew writing, in Exodus, Deuteronomy, Ecclesiastes, Psalms, and Proverbs, is devoted to the importance of obeying family rules. In India, too, the earliest codified literature (the *Rig-Veda*, about the last half of the 2nd millenium B.C., and the Law of Manu, about the beginning of the Christian Era) devote great attention to the family.

From time to time, imaginative social analysts or philosophers have sketched out plans for societies that *might* be created—utopias—in which new definitions of family roles are presented as solutions to traditional social problems. Plato's *Republic* is illustrative of this approach. He was probably the first to urge the creation of a society in which all people, men and women alike, would have an equal opportunity to develop their talents to the utmost, and to achieve a position in society solely through merit. Since family relations in all known societies prevent a selection based solely on individual worth, in Plato's utopia the tie between parents and children would play no part, because no one would know who was his own child or parent. Conception would take place at the same times each year at certain hymeneal festivities. Children born out of season would be eliminated (along with those born defective); all children would be taken from their parents at birth, and reared under challenging conditions by specially designated people. Similarly, experimental or utopian communities, like Oneida, the Shakers, and the Mormons in this country, insisted that changes in family relations were necessary to achieve their goals.

Included among the aims of many revolutions since the French Revolution of 1789 has been a profound alteration in family relations. Since World War II, the leaders of all countries undergoing industrialization have introduced new laws, well ahead of public opinion, intended to create family patterns that would be more in conformity with the demands of urban and industrial life.

All these facts, by demonstrating that philosophers, reformers, and religions, as well as secular leaders, have throughout history been at least implicitly aware of the importance of family patterns as a central element in the social structure, also suggest that the social analyst must understand family behavior in order to understand social processes generally.

The strategic significance of the family is to be found in its *mediating* function in the larger society. It links the *individual* to the larger social structure. A society will not survive unless its many needs are met, such as the production and distribution of food, protection of the young and old, the sick and the pregnant, conformity to the law, the socialization of the young, and so on. Only if *individuals* are motivated to serve the needs of the society will it be able to survive. The formal agencies of social control (such as the police) are not enough to do more than force the extreme deviant to conform. Socialization makes most of us wish to conform, but throughout each day we are often tempted to deviate. Thus both the internal controls and the formal authorities are insufficient. What is needed is a set of social forces that responds to the individual whenever he does well or poorly, supporting his internal controls as well as the controls of the formal agencies. The family, by surrounding the individual through much of his social life, can furnish that set of forces.

The family then, is made up of individuals, but it is also part of the larger social network. Thus we are all under the constant supervision of our kin, who feel free to criticize, suggest, order, cajole, praise, or threaten, so that we will

2

carry out our role obligations. Even in the most industrialized and urban of societies, where it is sometimes supposed that people lead rootless and anonymous lives, most people are in frequent interaction with other family members. Men who have achieved high position usually find that even as adults they still respond to their parents' criticisms, are still angered or hurt by a brother's scorn.

Thus it is *through the family* that the society is able to elicit from the *individual* his necessary contribution. The family, in turn, can continue to exist only if it is supported by the larger society. If the society as a larger social system furnishes the family, as a smaller social system, the conditions necessary for its survival, these two types of systems must be interrelated in many important ways. The two main foci in this volume will be the relations among family members and the relations between the family and the society.

Preconceived Notions about the Family

Such a task presents many difficulties. One of the greatest lies in ourselves. We know too much about the family to be able to study it both objectively and easily. Our emotions are aroused quickly by the behavior of families, and we are likely to feel that family patterns other than our own are queer or improper. We are too prone to argue about what is *right*, rather than coolly to demonstrate what *is*. In addition, we have had an opportunity to observe many people engaged in family behavior, so that when we consider almost any generalization (such as "the lower social strata have a higher divorce rate than the upper") we can often find a specific experience that seems to refute the generalization. Thus our personal experience is really a narrow sample of the wide range of family behavior, but it is so vivid to us, that we are likely to see no reason to look for broader data with which to test it.

Our emotional involvement and reliance on individual experience often convince people that the findings of family sociology must be "obvious," since they deal with what we already know. Many "well known" beliefs about the family, however, are not well-grounded in fact. Others are only partly true, and require precise study in order to be understood better. One such belief is that "children hold the family together." In fact, most divorcing couples do not have children. But the most valid data now suggest, rather, that the causal nexus is this: People who have not become well adjusted, who for many reasons may be prone to divorce, are also less likely to have children.

Perhaps the need for testing apparently self-evident ideas about the family may be seen in another way. Suppose that a researcher in the field of the family had demonstrated the following set of facts. Would it have been worth doing? Or were the facts already known?

1. The present divorce rate in the U.S. is much higher than the rates in primitive societies, and higher than any other nation has ever experienced.

2. Because of the importance of the extended family in China and India, the average size of the household has always been very high, with many generations living under one roof.

3. In Western nations, the age at marriage among peasants was always low, since early marriage meant that children would soon be produced, and these were useful in farming. By contrast, the average age at marriage among the nobility was generally higher.

Although these statements sound plausible to many people, and impressive arguments could be adduced to support them, in fact they are all false. A majority of primitive societies have higher rates of marital dissolution than our own, and several nations in the past have at various times equaled or exceeded our present rate—notably Japan in the 1880's, when even her official rate (certainly an underestimate) was over 300 divorces per 1,000 marriages. Every survey of Chinese and Indian households has shown that they are relatively small (about 3.3 to 5.5, from one region to another). Peasant marriages were later, on the average, than the nobility, requiring as they did that the couple have land of their own.

Thus we see that in the instances just cited, common beliefs *did* require testing. Of course, many popular beliefs about how families work *are* correct, but we cannot simply assume their correctness. We must examine many of our individual observations to see how well they fit other societies or perhaps the different family types in our own society.

To understand family behavior we must be self-conscious in our method. We n ust adopt an approach that will yield reliable results. Vast tables of figures, such as the ages of all the married couples in the world, taken from national censuses, would contain many facts, but might add very little to our grasp of family behavior. What we seek is *organized* facts, or a structure of propositions, that will illuminate one another. That is, we seek theory as well as facts. Theory without facts is blind speculation; facts without theory are random and often insignificant observations.

The Family as a Unique Institution

A brief consideration of certain peculiarities of the family as an element of the social structure will suggest how better theory and a fruitful general approach are needed in this area.

The family is the only social institution other than religion which is *formally* developed in all societies. Indeed, the term, "social structure" in anthropology is often used to mean the family and kinship structure. By contrast, some have argued that in certain societies legal systems do not exist because there is no formally organized legislative body or judiciary. Of course, it is possible to abstract from concrete behavior the legal *aspects* of action, or the economic aspects, or the political dynamics, even when there are no explicitly labeled agencies formally in control of these areas in the society. However, the kinship statuses and their responsibilities are the object of both formal and informal attention in societies at a high or a low technological level.

Family duties are the *direct* role responsibility of everyone in the society, with rare exceptions. Almost everyone is both born into a family and founds one of his own. Each person is kinsman to many. Many people, on the other hand, may escape the religious duties which others take for granted, or the political burdens of the society. Almost no family role responsibilities can be delegated to others, as more specialized obligations can be in a work situation.

Participation in family activities has a further interesting quality, that though it is not backed by the formal punishments supporting many other kinds of obligations, almost everyone takes part nonetheless. We must, for example, engage in economic or productive acts, or face the alternative of starving. We must enter the army, pay taxes, and appear before courts, or face physical penalties and force. However, no such penalties face the individual who does not wish to marry, or refuses to talk with his father or brother. Nevertheless, so pervasive and recurrent are the social pressures, and so intertwined with indirect or direct rewards and punishments, that almost everyone either conforms, or claims to conform, to family demands.

Next, as suggested earlier, the family is the fundamental *instrumental* foundation of the larger social structure, in that all other institutions depend on its contributions. The role behavior that is learned within the family becomes the model or prototype for role behavior required in other segments of

4

the society. The content of the socialization process is the cultural traditions of the society; by passing them on to the next generation the family acts as a conduit or transmission belt by which the culture is kept alive.

Next, each individual's total range of behavior, how he budgets his time and energies, is more easily visible to the family than to outsiders. Family members can evaluate how the individual is allocating his time and money in various of his role activities. Consequently, the family acts as a source of pressure on him to adjust—to work harder and play less, or go to church less and study his school lessons more. In all these ways, the family is an instrument or agent of the larger society; its failure to perform adequately means that the goals of the larger society may not be attained effectively.

A further striking characteristic of the family is that its major functions are separable from one another, but in fact are not separated in any known family system. These functions will be discussed in various contexts in this book, and need no great elaboration at this point. The family contributes these services to the society: reproduction of the young, physical maintenance of family members, social placement of the child, socialization, and social control. Clearly, all these activities could be separated. The mother could send her child to be fed in a neighborhood mess hall, and of course some harassed mothers do send their children to buy lunch in a local snack bar. Those who give birth to a child need not socialize the child. They might send the child to specialists, and indeed specialists do take more responsibility for this task as the child grows older. Parents might, as some eugenicists have suggested, be selected for their breeding qualities, but these might not include any great talent for training the young. Status-placement might be accomplished by random drawing of lots, by IQ tests or periodic examinations in physical and intellectual skills, or by polls of popularity, without regard to an individual's parents, those who socialized or fed him, or others who controlled his daily behavior.

Separations of this kind have been suggested from time to time, and a few hesitant attempts have been made here and there in the world to put them into operation. However, three conclusions relevant to this kind of division can be made. (1) In all known societies, the *ideal* (with certain qualifications to be noted) is that the family be entrusted with all these functions. (2) When one or more family tasks are entrusted to another agency by a revolutionary or utopian society, the change can be made only with the support of much ideological fervor, and sometimes political pressure as well. (3) These instances are also characterized by a gradual return to the more traditional type of family. In both the Israeli *kibbutzim* and the Russian experiments in relieving parents of child care, the ideal of completely communal living was urged, in which husband and wife were to have only a personal and emotional tie and not be bound to each other by constraint. The children were to see their parents at regular intervals but look to their nursery attendants and mother-surrogates for affection and direction during work hours. Each individual was to contribute his best skills to the cooperative unit without regard to family ties or sex status (i.e., there would be few or no "female" or "male" tasks). That ideal was maintained for a while, but behavior has gradually dropped away from the ideal. The only other country in which the pattern has been attempted on a large scale is China. Whether the Chinese commune will retreat from its high ambitions remains to be seen, but chances are good that it will follow the path of the *kibbutz* and the Russian *kolkhoz*.

Various factors contribute to such a deviation from the ideal, but the two most important sets of pressures cannot easily be separated from each other. First is the problem, also noted by Plato, that individuals who develop their

5

own attitudes and behaviors in the usual Western (i.e., European and European-based) family system do not adjust to the problems of the communal "family." The second is the likelihood that when the family is radically changed, the various relations between it and the larger society are changed, so that new strains are created, demanding new kinds of adjustments on the part of the individuals in the society. Perhaps the planners must develop somewhat different agencies, or a different blueprint, to transform the family.

Concretely, some of the factors reported as "causing" a deviation from the ideal of family living are the following. Some successful or ambitious men and women wish to break away from group control, and leave to establish their lives elsewhere. There, of course, they do not attempt to develop a communal pattern of family living. Parents do try to help their own children secure advantages over other children, where this is possible. Parents not only feel unhappy at not being with their children often enough (notice that youngsters need not "be home for meals"!), but perhaps some feel the husband-wife relationship itself is somewhat empty because children do not occupy in it their usually central place. Husband and wife usually desire more intimacy than is granted under communal arrangements. Finally, the financial costs of taking care of children outside the family are rather high.

These comments have nothing to do with "capitalism" in its current political and economic argument with "communism." It merely describes the historical fact that though various experiments in separating the major functions of the family from one another have been conducted, none simply evolved slowly from a previously existing family system; and the two modern important instances represent a retreat from the ideals of a previous generation. It is possible that some functions can be more easily separated than others; or that some family systems (for example matrilineal systems, to be discussed later) might lend themselves to a separation of functions more easily than others. Nevertheless, we have to begin with the data available now. Even cautiously interpreted, they suggest that the family is a rather stable institution.

A Sociological Approach to Family Research

The unusual features the family exhibits as a type of social sub-system require that some attention be paid to the approach to be used in studying it. First, neither ideal nor reality can be excluded from focus. It would, for example, be naive to suppose that because one-fourth to one-third of all couples marrying will eventually divorce, they do not cherish the ideal of monogamy. Kinsey estimated that about half of all married men engage in extra-marital intercourse, but perhaps nearly all these men believed in the ideal of faithfulness. On a more personal level, every reader of these lines has lied, but nevertheless most believe in the ideal of telling the truth.

A sociologist ascertains the ideals of family systems partly because they are a guide to behavior. Knowing that people believe in telling the truth, we can expect them to do so unless there are advantages in telling a lie, and we can even (as a manipulative measure) create the conditions under which people are more likely to tell the truth. We know also that when an individual violates the ideal, he is likely to conceal the violation, to find some internal excuse for the violation, and to be embarrassed if others find him out.

A sociologist may also be interested in ideals as values, as sets of norms which are passed on from one generation to another as a major constituent of culture. The organization of values, how norms in different areas change or are translated into a different form, how they are qualified by still other norms—all these are legitimate questions for a sociologist.

6

Next, as an element in this approach, the sociology of the family cannot confine its conclusions only to contemporary, urban (or suburban) U.S. life. In order to reach conclusions of any merit, a sociologist must confront his speculations and hypotheses with data from other societies, whether these are past or present, industrial or nonindustrial, Asiatic or European. Data from the historical past, such as Periclean Athens or Imperial Rome, are not often used, because as yet no sociologically adequate account of their family systems has been written. However, some reference to customs and beliefs of the past yield a better understanding of the range of social behavior, and often serves to refute or qualify an observation that seems to be accurate. Similarly, the use of data from other contemporary societies helps in establishing conclusions about family systems that are not found at all in U.S. society, such as matrilineal systems or polygyny. Or, an apparently simple relationship may take a different form in other societies. For example, in the U.S., almost all first marriages are based on a love relationship, and few will admit that they married someone with whom they were not in love. However, when other societies are brought in for comparison, love may play a small or a considerable part in the marriage.

In some societies love is viewed as irrelevant to mate choice. In many societies love is seen as a threat to the control by family elders over who marries whom, and thus over family alliances, and the inheritance of property. Consequently, various social arrangements are to be found which prevent love from being a primary basis of mate choice.

Although it is possible to investigate other perspectives in this discussion, family patterns will here be analyzed *sociologically*. A full analysis of any concrete object is impossible. Everything can be analyzed from a great many vantage points, each of them yielding a somewhat different picture. Everything is infinitely complex. For this reason, any science limits its perspective, the character of its particular thin slice of infinity. A sociology of the family does not pretend to describe adequately the biological or even the psychological relations among members of a family. Each of these approaches has its own justification. The sociological approach focuses on the family as a social institution, the peculiar and unique quality of family interaction as *social*. Family systems exhibit the characteristics of legitimacy and authority, which are not biological categories at all. The values relating to the family, or the rights and duties of family statuses, such as father or daughter, are not psychological categories, but *are* peculiar to the theoretical level of sociology. Analysis of the personality cannot tell us much about the differences in family behavior between, say, China and Japan. Utilizing a consistently sociological approach misses some important information about concrete family interaction, but also yields some systematization, some rigor, by staying on one theoretical level.

In any event, if a sociologist moves from the sociological to the psychological level of theory, he should at least be conscious of it. And if the investigation turns to the impact of biological or psychological factors on the family, they should be examined with reference to their *social* meaning. For example, interracial marriage is of little biological significance, but of great social importance. A sociologist studying the family does not analyze the *psychodynamics* of mental disease, but is interested in the impact of mental disease on the social relations in a particular family or type of family, how different family types adjust to it, which kinds of family patterns or constellations are more likely to produce certain types of mental disease. The biological or psychological aspects of the family are not the province of the sociologist, except when he is investigating their social meaning.

7

biological
bases
of the family

two

Man's family patterns are determined in part by the peculiar task imposed on them: The family is the only social institution charged with transforming a biological organism into a human being. By the time other institutions begin to shape the individual in important ways, his family has already accomplished much of this transformation, having taught him to speak and to play out many social roles.

This close relation between family and biological factors suggests other reasons for considering the biological foundations of the family. The family is also charged with the social arrangements having to do with the biological factors of sex and reproduction. Next, if the family did not make adequate provision for the biological needs of man, obviously society would die out. In addition, kinship structure is a network of social roles linked by real or supposed biological relations. To understand the family better, then, it is worthwhile examining the biological material that is to be transformed.

Assessment of Data

In such an inquiry, various types of data are not available, and others are irrelevant, even though reputable scholars have sometimes used them in the past. It is not possible to outline the gradual evolution of man as a *biological* species, and to correlate it in any way with the gradual evolution of human *family* systems. We know nothing important, and shall know nothing, about this latter evolution prior to written history. The data are lost forever. Even with respect to purely biological evolution, our knowledge is entirely anatomical. We need instead some knowledge of the physiological evolution of man, of his endocrinal or hormonal changes, or perhaps some information about the quality of his mental behavior rather than the sheer size of his brain.

Nor do the family groupings of our four great ape cousins, the anthropoids, tell us what are the "purely biological" foundations of man's family patterns. The gorilla, orangutan, chimpanzee, and gibbon all branched apart from man's life of evolution during the Miocene Age, or perhaps the early Pliocene, about 30 million to 35 million years ago, according to some estimates, and thus are only very distant "cousins." More important, we have reliable field studies of family behavior among only two of these animals, the gibbon and the gorilla, and their domestic patterns seem dissimilar. Such sources cannot be ignored, but the exact relationship between such animal behavior and the biological heritage of man is not clear.

Another weak line of reasoning has attracted some investigators—that we might discover the semi-animal qualities of man by studying *contemporary* societies that use stone implements, such as the Australian aborigines. That is, modern stone-age societies would exhibit family patterns like those of the prehistoric Stone Age—i.e., the Paleolithic—when man had begun to branch away from his animal cousins. Thus we would be learning about very ancient social patterns as well as something about our animal beginnings.

Unfortunately, we do not know anything about the domestic behavior of Paleolithic Man, and there is no reason to suppose that the families of present-day stone-using people are similar to those of men who lived a hundred millennia ago. Studying Australian tribes tells us about their family patterns—valuable data indeed, but not to be trusted as a known or definte step in the evolution of man's family behavior. Consequently, it is not possible to ascertain the gradually changing relations of man's biological structure to his family structure over the past million years.

Moreover, other barriers to knowledge must be faced. We cannot learn the "purely biological" aspects of man by rearing infants in isolation from all human relations and then comparing their adult behavior with that of normally socialized adults.

At first, this might seem a promising direction of inquiry. The normal individual's biological patterns are changed by socialization. By the time we can observe the child or adult, some biological aspects of behavior have been altered in a wide range of areas, from tastes for food to sexual preferences. Therefore, it would seem, if we reared a child in total isolation, we might learn exactly what is contributed by biological factors; and if we reared several children in isolation, we might bring them together at adulthood and see what kinds of "families" they formed.

Aside from the humanitarian objections to such an experiment, however, it is self-contaminating. A child reared in social isolation does not seem to develop normally, and cannot function adequately *even as an animal*. This is also true, apparently, of monkeys. As to the so-called "wolf children," youngsters who have grown up with wild animals, the evidence suggests that none ever existed. Consequently, descriptions of their behavior cannot be used to speculate about what man's family behavior would be if he were not a social and cultural being, and were instead only a "biological animal."

Sociologists assert that one conclusion *can* be inferred from the cases of

9

isolated children as well as from many studies of socialization—that is, that human culture is not just a "thin veneer" covering the savage underneath. Both culture and biology transform each other in this species. This beast, man, *is* different. Nowhere does he live isolated, or purely as an animal. He cannot even develop normally as an animal without human contact and cultural experiences.

This area of inquiry is clouded by many polemics, precisely because man is like other animals in many ways, and biological explanations of human behavior seem simple although they are hard to demonstrate. A common observation is that "males are naturally polygynous," or "women should take care of children because they have a maternal instinct"; but sound counter-arguments can be leveled against such statements. Consequently, we should proceed cautiously in approaching these questions: (1) How much of family behavior can be explained by biological factors? (2) What peculiar biological traits of man as a species determine his family patterns? We may learn in time, as we accumulate more biological information, that man's biology has far more impact on his life than is now supposed; but that period cannot be anticipated now. A family pattern that *seems* "natural" may nevertheless be created by cultural and social factors. Thus, as a further problem in proof, a pattern that is common to all societies cannot therefore be assumed to be biological in character. All societies have religious systems, but almost certainly these are not biological in origin. All societies have family values that define some children as illegitimate, others as legitimate, but this pattern cannot be traced to biological factors. What seems most useful, then, is to look at the biological elements that seem most likely to affect human family behavior, but simply to treat this interaction as a problem that is far from being clearly understood.

Terminology and Definitions
Let us first clarify a few basic terms in this inquiry. *Socialization* is the process by which the young human being acquires the values and knowledge of his group and learns the social roles appropriate to his position in it. Since no other animal acquires culture, it is not proper to apply this term to animal learning. Animal behavior is complex, however, and made up of many processes. Both animals and man have *reflexes*, such as salivating when food is in the mouth, winking when a moving object suddenly threatens the eye, or (in human and ape infants) grasping any object the hand touches. These are innate sensory-motor responses, usually involving one part of the body. Some, like the salivating reflex, can be conditioned by learning, so that food smells or the ringing of a bell may arouse this behavioral pattern before any food is actually present.

Animals also have *drives*, which are impulses to satiate some hunger for food, water, or sex. The animal experiences a drive even if no outside stimulus is present, but has no "need" to pull away from a hot object (a reflex) if there is no such object present. The drive is a general striving toward some goal, but unlike the reflex it does not refer to any specific neural mechanisms by which the goal is reached.

We cannot assume that if a type of animal behavior appears later in life it must be due to learning, for some changes occur as a result of *maturation*. Many hormones (e.g., the sexual) appear in quantity only when the animal grows up. Many animals rarely depend on learning, yet do alter their behavior as their bodies mature. And, of course, some behavior (e.g., reproduction) is possible only after considerable maturation, whether or not learning itself is of great importance in the animal's life. It is especially important that these elements in animal behavior be separated from *instincts*, since man's biological

10

heritage apparently contains them all, except instincts. This assertion depends, of course, partly on the definition of the term. Research over the past generation has shown that learning is of more significance in animal life than once was assumed, and the term has come to mean, not simply any goal-adapted behavior, but a fairly complex behavior-linkage, in which the animal moves towards a goal through a sequence of related acts but without much prior learning. Thus the *drive* is different, since it does not contain the mechanisms for its own solution. The reflex may form the building block of instincts, but any single reflex is but an automatic neural response to a stimulus. The instinct is made up of both the stimulus (temperature, time of year, the presence of another animal) and the internal state of the animal (level of sex drive, hunger) and is executed through a chain of acts linked together somewhat automatically. The hanging nest of the Baltimore Oriole, or the migration behavior of birds, would be ascribed to an instinct. Yet apparently all instincts can be modified somewhat by learning; for example, the Oriole now uses machine-made threads in its nest.

Biological vs. Cultural Factors

Man thus depends more on learning than does any other animal and cannot develop normally without social contact. The family is the social invention that copes partially with the problem of transforming a biological organism into a human being. What the family does and how it operates tells us something about the contribution or the strain created by the *physical* qualities of man when they are pressed into a *cultural* mold. One limit which man's organic traits place on the culture and the family is that the society cannot ask the biologically impossible of its members. The religious system may define some people as members of a Kangaroo totem, and thus spiritually as kangaroos, but even in the midst of religious ceremonies these people cannot really *become* kangaroos. Women must bear the children in all societies. Twins may be viewed as semi-sacred, but not every woman can be expected to bear twins.

As a second step in understanding the interaction between biological factors and the human family, it is self-evident that the society and the family must assure adequate conditions for replacing each generation. Food must be procured and distributed to the young, the old, the ill, and the disabled. Individuals must be protected against predators, marauding bands, and the vagaries of climate. Where possible, medical help must be obtained. These tasks are the responsibility of family members.

However, these statements must not be interpreted to mean that the closest possible harmony and balance between biological and social needs have occurred over thousands of generations by some kind of natural evolution in which the best possible fit between the two was achieved. Obviously, within fairly wide limits some harmony must exist, or else the species would die out. On the other hand, the culture may place great demands on the biological organism. Among the Plains Indians, individuals who sought visions would undergo starvation and self-torture. In other societies people have been required to submit to scarification, tatooing, circumcision, and subincision. In perhaps all societies, some people are asked at times to risk their lives for the group. Mothers and fathers are expected to protect their young even if they might die in the attempt.

Moreover, the biological organism in turn imposes strains on the cultural norms. That is, it makes conformity to those norms difficult. The norms require considerable control over the time, place, and occasion for defecation, urination, coughing, and belching, and impose restrictions on the satisfaction of hunger, sex, or thirst drives as well as over the immediate impulses to murder that we sometimes feel.

That is, the family does not work with an infinitely plastic organism. It is a particular kind of animal, which cannot adjust to every possible type of animal society. In turn, cultures are not infinitely variant, in spite of their apparently wide range of types. Many societies can be conceived that have perhaps never existed, and science fiction has sketched some of these over the past half-century. Not all such societies are sociologically possible.

In interpreting man's behavior, a sociologist focuses on man's cultural and social patterns, because these are his area of inquiry. With reference to all aspects of human behavior, however, it is meaningless to assert that the biological is less or more important than the cultural, just as it is to argue that hydrogen or oxygen are more important in producing the unique qualities of water. A cautious formulation would simply be that man's biological traits make his family systems possible and set some limits to their variation, and we do not know as yet how narrow those limits are. In any event, as we shall see, the special focus of sociology on human norms and values, on cultural and linguistic behavior, on legitimacy and morality—in short, on behavior that *cannot* be explained biologically—requires us merely to understand the major points at which the animal qualities of man seem to affect family action. Man's uniqueness as a creator and bearer of culture is without question. On the other hand, man has almost no *unique* biological traits (indeed, perhaps none) that shape his family patterns in important ways. In all significant biological aspects, he differs from his nearest ape cousins, the anthropoids, in degree only. His most conspicuous relevant trait, his large and complex brain, permits him to make symbols and to reason abstractly, but whether this is a true *qualitative* distinction or only a quantitative one, is difficult to prove by rigorous experiment. Certainly some animal psychologists would argue that the matter is not yet settled.

Let us review the animal traits that seem most important in shaping man's family life.

Like many other animals, man is helpless at birth, and would die quickly without care. Unlike most, however, man is also unable to care for himself at several years of age. This characteristic is linked with several others to form a complex that sets man apart. (1) Man matures later than any other animal, (2) has no instincts to simplify his adjustment to the environment, and (3) possesses the most complex brain among all animals.

At what age a human child might survive alone is a subject primarily for speculation. Large grazing animals such as elephants, most whales, hippopotamuses, and rhinoceroses, mature physically rather slowly, but within a few days after birth can forage for themselves, even while living mainly from their mothers' milk. If alone, they may be more easily killed, but even at a few months of age they can find their own food. Predators, of course, cannot, since they have to learn hunting skills, but within a year they too could live independently if they had to.

Man cannot. His physical equipment is inadequate in all respects, and simple physical maturation does not automatically confer enough skill on him. No instincts impel him to build a shelter, to kill other animals, to grow plants, or to create tools. His reflexes, such as winking his eye when an object suddenly looms close, or recoiling swiftly when burned, will save him from some dangers. His hunger and thirst drives will impel him to action and to some accidental solutions, but even at five or six years of age man's physical achievements and endowments seem insufficient to enable him to survive alone.

One might, then, view culture as an evolutionary adaptation to a large

biological bases of the family

brain and the lack of instincts; or the lack of instincts may be attributed to man's no longer needing them, after he developed a large brain and culture. The modern theory of the evolution of man asserts that the size of man's brain is the result of the usual process of evolution, the survival of the "fittest," by which those who learned culture most easily survived better, compared not with other animals, but compared with other, less brainy, human beings.

For these reasons, man *must* live in some sort of family grouping, to be fed, protected, and taught what nature has not provided. Given such a social environment in his early years, however, man is a formidable beast, able to kill the largest and most savage animals. From a period estimated at half a million to a million years ago, man, or his man-like ancestors, has left scattered over the earth large deposits of bones from a wide range of large and small mammals (including man himself) that have fallen victim to his skill. His complex brain permits him to learn and discover more quickly, and to supplement his insufficient physical equipment with weapons to crush, slash, and stab.

The Sex Factor

Man must learn all the behavioral patterns of family life, from sexual intercourse to caring for children. Perhaps more important are two implications of such a brain. One is that experience may create associations or conditioned responses that link the sex drive to almost any object or situation. In our own society, for example, the sex drive comes to be related to perfume, flowers, certain types of music, words and particular ways or tones of expression, gestures, and a wide variety of social situations defined as sexual to some degree. A moment's thought about these is enough to remind us that they are not *intrinsically* sexual, and a list from our society would not be the same as a list from another society—e.g., different parts of the body have a different sexual meaning from one society to another. These items have, as it were, become sexualized by a lifetime of cultural conditioning.

Thus this particular biological element, the complex brain, opens the possibility of inhibiting the sexual drive, and shaping it by many different types of social stimuli.

Another way of phrasing this is to say that as one compares the lower mammals to the higher, or the lower primates to the higher, the sexual impulse becomes more *social*, more dependent on learning. A rhesus monkey reared through adolescence away from other monkeys will not be able to engage adequately in normal mating behavior.

Correspondingly, many patterns of behavior come to have a sexual meaning, or more generally a familial meaning. For example, in societies that practice mother-in-law avoidance, for a son-in-law to speak to her is viewed as worse than bad manners, perhaps even bordering on the sexually improper.

Conversely, the sex drive itself is shaped, channeled, and restricted in all societies through the complex learning potential of our brain. Some people who might be physically attractive and geographically available—for example, sisters and brothers—come to be viewed as impossible sex partners, who arouse no conscious sex desire at all. We learn to feel shame, guilt, and embarrassment when our sex drive causes us to break some of these norms. Certain situations cause us to lose any sex desire we might feel, because our socialization has effectively repressed these feelings. More broadly, our complex neural mechanism permits a rich conditioning to occur, by which only certain familial behavioral patterns seem right or desirable.

Another important biological trait is the relative constancy of man's sex drive. Unlike most animals, the human female has no rutting season. The female has a menstrual cycle, not an estrus cycle. It is not even certain that a definite cycle of sex desire parallels the menstrual cycle. At approximately the midpoint of this cycle, the female is fertile, but not even a majority of women report an increase in desire at this time. Many in fact say they feel such an increase at the time of menstruation—perhaps because they have less fear of pregnancy then, and thus feel the sex drive more intensely. Sex desire may vary because of many factors, from stomach aches to the visit of a mother-in-law, but the healthy human adult may feel such a desire at any phase of the menstrual cycle.

This general biological factor—the desire of the two sexes to continue to associate intimately with each other—has important consequences for the family. From a *biological* point of view, the family may be said to be made up of a close tie between mother and child, and one between the mother and the father. There is no evidence of any *paternal drive*, but the male remains in the family grouping because of his complex socio-sexual relations with the female.

A minor biological characteristic is that the human female typically bears *one* child at a time, rather than a litter. This permits a rather intense focus of socialization pressures on the infant, and lessens somewhat the burden on the parents. It also increases the intensity of the emotional tie between mother and child, and thus facilitates the socialization process.

Perhaps the most obscure area of biological effects on the human family is that of sex differences. This debate has doubtless engaged men's attention for thousands of years, and the modern accumulation of scientific evidence makes it clear that many apparent differences may be due to social conditioning. Almost certainly, for example, the superiority of girls in language skills and of boys in mechanical skills does not grow from biological differences.

Confining ourselves to the sex differences that seem relevant to family patterns, the most prominent is that the female menstruates, bears the children, and lactates. It is easy, but inexcusably loose, to infer that "therefore" the woman must remain close to the hearth, "should" engage in women's tasks, or that women's and men's roles differ because of these factors. Menstruation does reduce the woman's capacity to work, but it occurs only once a month, and women in all societies continue to work during this period. It would, moreover, violate the facts to assert that men by contrast always work intensively. Similarly, pregnancy and childbearing do tire the female, and increase her mortality; but most men's tasks do not require great strength or endurance, while in most societies the pregnant woman is expected to work.

Biological traits need not determine *completely* so complex a family pattern as the division of labor. If they do no more than give the male an advantage in hunting, wandering, and war, they increase the likelihood that he *will* follow such pursuits. Of course, whatever the relative advantages, they do not allow us to infer that women *should* remain at home.

Perhaps in the same category is the male's greater strength and endurance. Weight for weight, the human male can beat the female in a fair fight. Men also reign dominant in all known societies; no matriarchy (i.e., a society ruled by women) is known to exist. This fact is not a simple inference from the relative muscular strength of the two sexes, since the authority of dominance is based on the acceptance of a *value* system, which is not a biological trait. Woman of a higher class or caste may give orders to males of a lower class or caste, without regard to who has the biggest muscles. Possibly women might *keep* a dominant position through effective socialization backed by a religious system that required women to be venerated. On the other hand, how such a system might evolve is

14

not clear. Force plays an important role in the establishment of authority, and here men seemingly have always held the advantage.

One widely accepted difference should be viewed sceptically until it is more fully clarified—the supposedly later maturation of males. There is no evidence that girls produce a viable egg any earlier than boys produce a viable sperm cell. Different parts of the body grow at different rates of speed in boys and girls at different times. In middle adolescence the long bones of the body grow faster in boys than in girls, while about the time of puberty girls will be (on the average) slightly taller than boys. However, since some changes continue to occur in both throughout the 'teens, the problem of deciding when the individual is physically mature is difficult at best, and there are no accepted criteria by which to test the notion that women mature earlier.

The popular belief seems to be based on a *social* rather than a physical definition. The girl of 15 years is no more "ready for childbirth" than is a boy of the same age. Indeed, biologically she is less ready, since her immature body might be harmed by the experience, and the boy's is certain not to be. The girl is, on the other hand, more likely to be able to discharge the minimal tasks of housekeeper-mother than a boy is to handle the tasks of job-holder and father. Notice, however, that these are *social* definitions, and indicate that if the boy of 15 is less mature socially, less close to being able to discharge adult role obligations, it is because society demands far more of him.

In another area, too, that of dating, social definitions are dominant. To be a desirable dating companion to older males, a 15-year-old girl need be only pretty, charming, and possessed of the typical secondary sex characteristics of her age. A 15-year-old boy with the same development of secondary male sex traits (e.g., beginnings of a beard) is defined as a barely acceptable date for such a girl, and he is socially defined as inacceptable for an older girl.

That is, the popular definitions of "maturity" are not based on the *physical* differences in maturation between the sexes, but on the differing social roles they are to fill.

A further difference that is less important for family structures than for subtle areas of psychological interaction is that the male must feel some sexual desire in order to engage in sexual intercourse, and must experience an orgasm in order to impregnate the female, but the female may become pregnant without any such sensations. Some have argued that therefore intercourse is more of a psychological challenge to the male; it is a potential failure, a possible risk to his masculinity.

Certainly the male in Western society does experience this anxiety at times, and male resistance in some countries to the use of contraceptives (a significant hindrance to birth-control campaigns) is interpreted by some analysts as in part a wish or need to prove masculinity by keeping the wife pregnant.

Possibly this difference appears in another aspect of male-female relations, the lesser evaluation given in most societies to the woman's pleasure in sexual intercourse. For the purposes of continuing a family, lineage, or society, her enjoyment of sex is unimportant, and all that is necessary is that she submit. It is to be emphasized that no evidence exists that shows women are biologically incapable of as intense desires or orgasmic experiences as men. What is relevant is that one important function of the family, reproduction, can be taken care of without the development of sentiments or social patterns designed to arouse and satisfy sex desires in women.

Here the biological factors parallel the social definitions in certain ways. The male is stronger and can protect himself better than the female against external dangers, and is also permitted and encouraged to venture, to explore, and to take initiative, more than the female. In courtship practices the male is also given the initiative—and, from a biological view this is the more necessary, since for reproductive purposes *his* desire is the more important factor.

The biological nexus between mother and fetus is obvious; that between mother and child remains obscure and a topic of debate among social scientists. Though maternal behavior is learned in the socialization process, it is also shaped or limited somewhat by biological factors that at least increase the chances of a close emotional tie between mother and child. Both derive some tactile pleasure and warmth from the physical contact. The infant enjoys nursing, the satisfaction of its hunger drive. Both gain some satisfaction from the suckling process. It is also likely that in the post-parturition period the responses of the female are made more maternal because of hormonal secretions. Injection of certain female hormones in lower animals can induce "mothering" behavior, but adequate experimental evidence on human females is not yet available. These factors do not make the social of any less importance, but do increase the likelihood of close, continuing, emotional interaction between mother and child—necessary elements in the foundations of the family.

Biosocial Factors

These biological factors are relatively few, and do not explain even the main peculiarities of human family life. Further limits to the variation in family behavior are set by another set of patterns that may be called "biosocial." They are found generally among the mammals, all of which are social. They do not depend on culture. They are not "taught," or do not need to be, and yet are not instincts. They are characteristics we share with other mammals, and though among human beings they are given form and force by culture, it seems nevertheless likely that their foundations are biological. Or, phrased another way, they are so much a part of our biological heritage that to eliminate them by contrary cultural patterns would be difficult.

First, there is a family grouping of some kind—e.g., in a pride of lions, an adult male, one or more adult females, adolescents, and whelps; among gibbons, an adult male and female, together with adolescents and still younger gibbons. It may be composed of essentially two kinds of strong biological ties, between adult male and female, and between the mother and her offspring. But this grouping is not a random association of animals, lasting only a few days or months. Some shifts in membership do occur, but the group is identifiable, and may persist for years and through the birth and maturation of several sets of offspring.

Closely related is a second biosocial trait, territoriality. Each such group occupies a definite space, large enough for an adequate food supply. Its members usually defend their territory successfully from invaders of the same species (they *must* do so, to survive). Invasion and defense often consist more in threatening behavior than combat, but when real incursions occur even fairly peaceable animals become savage fighters. Family groupings do not simply adopt a pattern of wandering indiscriminately in and through one another's space. Here biological needs are linked closely with the needs of the family. Each species requires a varying amount of space, depending on the richness of the food supply, for the sustenance of a family grouping. In addition, each family grouping learns the location of different foods in a given area, and would thus be handicapped in feeding if it were displaced. Normally, the adult male or males engage most in defense of the territory. On the other hand, if the food supply is especially rich, and the population low, the territory may be less vig-

16

orously defended. Gorillas, for example, live under such conditions, and their groupings may mingle casually for a day or so, with only a few gestures of latent attack between the great silver-backed adult males.

A similar pattern, but one more closely tied to family behavior, is that of jealousy—often in the female, perhaps always in the male. Jealousy may play a part in territoriality, since sometimes the invader is alone and may threaten to supplant the mate of one of the adults in the invaded grouping.

It is not necessary to give a cultural or moral interpretation to this behavior. The adult male tries to kill or drive off any adult male that attempts to approach sexually "his" mate or mates. If the animals are migratory, and the females have not arrived as yet in the mating area (e.g., sea lions), the same behavior is observable, taking the form of defending a particular territory. Loss of the area means loss of the *mates*, rather than food. Ample space and food are available, but the females return to an *area*, and thus to the male who holds it. Among gibbons, both males and females exhibit a jealousy pattern. This reaction does not determine all the peculiarities of human jealousy, but does suggest that not all of man's jealousy comes from a thin veneer of culture. On the other hand, the behavior of the gorilla in the wild seems to exhibit little or no jealousy.

A final biosocial trait is that of hierarchy or dominance. A group of mammals is not a simple aggregate, but it has a structure. One of its traits is a "pecking order"—in one form, animal A gives way before animal B, who gives way before C, and so on, to the dominant animal, who gives way to no one. Among most mammals, this dominant animal is an adult male. Many complexities of structure occur, and the hierarchy shifts at times. For example, an adolescent subordinate male may eventually become dominant.

Such a hierarchy is essentially a learned set of expectations. In its crudest form, animal A learns that if he stands his ground, or will not yield a bit of fruit or meat, he will be slashed or pummeled by B. One result is more *order*, if less justice. Each animal knows to which other animal he must yield food or the right of way. If the dominant male starts to leave, the others follow, thus keeping the group together. The group will follow only this animal. If two juveniles make a great disturbance, a dominant animal may cuff one or both. It is not necessarily the strongest or most intelligent who is dominant. Aggressiveness, the readiness to attack, often weighs more heavily, as indeed is so often the situation among human beings. It is important here not to extrapolate from a biosocial trait such as dominance, to the culturally *approved authority* patterns of the human family. In both, it is the adult male parent who is given this privilege, but among animals it is not based on any system of cultural values, or "right." This does not exhaust the matter, since it is possible that if the cultural pattern did not exist then, *some* pattern of hierarchy would exist if only to achieve order, and in most cases the top animal would be the male parent. Or, in simple terms, he would be, on the average, stronger and more enduring, not interrupted in his aggressiveness by menstruation, bearing children, or lactation, and oriented more commonly toward protecting the group from outside marauders; and in most conflicts with members of his own group he would win.

Perhaps one might assert, almost in contrast, that it is less striking that most, perhaps all, family systems bestow this moral privilege on the male parent, as though it were ultimately a biosocial trait; and rather more striking that the various value patterns in human societies do *not* permit the male to use all possible force to subdue others in his family. He enjoys the authority derived from culture, but is also *restricted* in his use of coercion to control others in his family.

17

These essentially biological patterns limit the forms that the human family can take. At the same time, however, they cannot transform the biological organism into a human being—i.e., an actor moved by values and norms, able to communicate, and intent on preserving a cultural heritage. Moreover, they do not explain the *specific* complexities of family structures. At most, they serve as a foundation on which human kinship networks and values might be constructed.

The Link between the Biological and Cultural

In order to go beyond the biological to the cultural, it is necessary to find a link through which the two are indissolubly connected. This may be found in the particular dependence of the *biological* on the role relations imposed by the culture. The crucial result of the socialization process is that individuals come to *want* to do the tasks that *must* be done if the society and its members are to survive. They are motivated to gain various kinds of personal satisfaction from carrying out their role obligations, such as caring for their children or teaching them something of their religious heritage, while these tasks also contribute ultimately to the continuance of the society. Within their role networks, they also receive punishments or rewards for fulfilling these obligations, which are mostly *not* to society, but to particular individuals or groups.

This means that for an individual infant to survive, and thus the society itself, he must be socialized; and one or more individuals must also *want* to socialize him. This in turn means that these persons must have been socialized themselves, when *they* were young, to want to socialize their children. This structural relation, linking *three* generations, by which one generation socializes a second to want to socialize the third, is a necessary link between the cultural and the biological heritage. Merely to teach the young the necessary cultural conduct for the society would not maintain the culture, if it did not include the moral injunction to teach each generation to teach the succeeding one.

The human family possesses several characteristics that facilitate socialization. It lasts a relatively *long* time, because human beings *biologically* have a long life (relative to other animals) and because of the ties between its members. This gives a fuller opportunity for transmitting the cultural traditions of the society to the child. The mother-child tie is emotionally intimate, which also facilitates socialization. In addition, the pattern of dominance gives further authority to what is learned; that is, the authority and greater force commanded by parents make their lessons more impressive to the child.

However, this linking of the biological and the cultural through the necessity of including in the socialization content the motivation not only to socialize the next generation, but also to socialize *that* generation to socialize the next, requires that these role obligations become fixed and specified for a particular person or persons. The obligation must be anchored in a specific unit. What that unit must be is not clear, but it must last a long time, to care for an animal that is helpless for many years. It must contain an adult female, to bear and nurse the child. It must be linked by dominance (threats of force) and affection, to facilitate socialization. Conceivably, the society might create special units to take over all but the reproductive function, but even the Israeli *kibbutz*, the Chinese commune, and the Soviet nurseries have attempted no more than a partial acceptance of all these duties, and no denial of most parental rights or duties.

18

legitimacy
and illegitimacy
three

The infant human animal cannot survive unless adults have been socialized to care for it. This is the key link between the biological survival of the individual organism, and the social system of the family, between the biological survival of the human species, and the transmission of the culture from one generation to the next. The culture cannot continue unless it can cope with the problems of human biological survival.

As mentioned in the last chapter, the crucial link in this interdependence is that the child is taught not only to want to rear children but also to rear his children *in turn* so that they want to take care of *their* children. Thereby, biological continuity is assured, through the cultural patterns transmitted in the socialization process.

The Key Role of Socialization

How was this link established? Social control over child care and thus over the *social unit* responsible for it has become more important precisely to the extent that the human animal in its evolution has come to depend increasingly on culture and not on its instincts or drives. That is, the human community and its culture have come to depend on the effectiveness of socialization—i.e., how well the child acquires the values, attitudes, or behaviors

19

of his community and family. Consequently, the community must shape or guide the unit that passes on the values to its next generation.

Just when this evolutionary shift occurred, from a dependence on biological patterns to a dependence on cultural patterns; from little or no community concern over who mated whom, or over the effectiveness of child care, to systems of marriages arranged by parents, is shrouded in the past. It seems clear, however, that increasing dependence on socialization required the human community to control more fully the choice of mate as well as the subsequent family behavior of the couple. One form this control took was the disapproval of casual sexual unions which created a child without a family unit responsible for it. Those who established such a unit would have to be either mature enough to support themselves and their children, or be linked with another family unit such as an extended household, which contained enough adults to care for the next generation of children.

This heightened concern with who might mate with whom, and with the cultural content passed on to the next generation, increased as the independence and complexity of cultural patterns increased. In other words, as men came to be more dependent on culture, and any given cultural item became more significant in its relation to *other* cultural items than to biological survival, man came to control the formation and operation of the unit—the family—that was responsible for transmitting that culture to the next generation.

In some past era, then, man's greater dependence on his culture pressed him to establish *rules of legitimacy*—i.e., regulations that define who has the right to procreate and rear a fully accepted member of the society. These rules determine the *social placement* of the child. Until that decision has been made, no decisions can be made concerning its physical care of socialization.

Thus legitimacy—and *therefore* illegitimacy—is a fundamental characteristic of the human family, shared by no other animal grouping, and is a central concept for understanding family behavior. It is for these reasons that we now consider various of its aspects.

Legitimacy and Role Obligations

By determining the social placement of the child, the rules of legitimacy help to define the role obligations of adults to the child. The infant is a symbol of many important role relations among adults. It indicates an intimacy between parents, and its existence makes continuing demands on a network of adults. These adults, in turn, make demands on one another because of the child. If the child has no acknowledged father, or the "wrong" father, these obligations are ambiguous or unmet, or run counter to already established duties. The already married father of an illegitimate child cannot take care of it without failing to some extent in his obligations to this own family, even if he is wealthy. The child whose parents are not married does not belong to the father's family, and neither the father nor his family needs to meet more than minimal legal obligations to the child. The child's position is ambiguous, and its socialization experience is likely to be inadequate. In short, it is the consequences for adults, for the society, more than for the child, which the rules against illegitimacy are supposed to prevent. For these reasons, illegitimacy is more of a scandal than premarital sexual intercourse, even when the latter is also disapproved. Every society controls to some extent who may mate with whom, and disapproves of bearing children casually or as the accidental result of a sexual encounter. Far more control is exerted over who may produce children than over who may "date" whom.

legitimacy and illegitimacy

To focus on illegitimacy, then, does not betray a value judgment on the part of the social analyst, but is required by the importance it assumes for the form and meaning of the family structure. The society must be concerned with social placement or jeopardize its continuity. It is no paradox, then, to assert that the placement of the future child is considered in any decision concerning who may marry whom.

This importance was emphasized more than a generation ago by Bronislaw Malinowski, who enunciated an apparently social rule, the Principle of Legitimacy, according to which "no child should be brought into the world without a man—and one man at that—assuming the role of sociological father. . . ." That is, every society has a rule stating that each child ought to have a sociological father. The focus of the rule may be seen clearly in the fact that about 60 per cent of the societies for which data are available permit premarital sexual relations, but even these sexually more permissive societies do not approve of childbirth outside the marital relationship. Marriage, then, bestows legitimacy on parenthood more than on sex. Consequently, Malinowski's Principle should properly be extended to *motherhood* as well.

A brief examination of this point shows more clearly the primary aim of the social rules for the establishment of a family—i.e., the rules of legitimacy. On the one hand, the social responsibility of the mother *is* less often in question, since the child is more obviously tied to her from the beginning of its life, than to the father. Her refusal to take that responsibility, however, would be viewed as more "unnatural," a more serious violation of role obligations, than the parallel refusal on the part of the father. In other words, perhaps the rule need not apply so specifically to the mother, since she is almost certain to be present anyway. It is the father who is more likely to be absent.

The difference suggests, however, that the various rules of legitimacy are more definitely focused on social placement, on *descent*, on the location of the child in the kinship network, than on whether the child is fed or nursed. If the child is socially located, it will very likely be cared for; but merely caring for it will not necessarily give it a social position. Consequently, we are led to amend Malinowski's general principle: The society will be less concerned with illegitimacy when it occurs in the lower social ranks, since their position is less significant for the larger social structure. In addition, it seems likely that in most societies the absence of the father might usually be more critical, because his is more likely to be the main line of descent; without a legal tie with the father, the child cannot be properly placed in the family system. Perhaps we might also expect that in a *matrilineal* system, in which descent is traced through the *mother*, there would be less concern about the exact identity of the biological father so long as the mother were married. The rules of marriage—i.e., who is permitted to marry whom—determine the social placement of the child, guarantee its socialization, and thus define both illegitimacy and legitimacy. The illegitimate child is a burden, with no benefit to its mother's kin, since his lack of a secure place in the kinship line means that his obligations to them are not firm or definite. They receive no gifts from the other kinship line, since there has been no marriage. The child represents, in some societies, a violation of the elders' power to decide and execute the marriage itself. Usually, there is no father to assume the social and economic care of the child, and the child is not an extension of the kinship line. Thus, the prohibition of illegitimacy is based on several supporting rules and consequences.

The various rules that determine who may marry whom define which types of births are legitimate or illegitimate. For this reason Kingsley Davis

21

comments that one reason for illegitimacy is marriage. If there were no rules, they would not be violated. Or, as Crane Brinton comments,

> Bastardy and marriage in this world are quite supplementary—you cannot have one without the other. In another world, you may indeed separate the two institutions and eliminate one of them either by having marriage so perfect—in various senses—that no one will ever commit fornication or adultery, or by having fornication so perfect that no one will ever commit marriage.[1]

Social Norms Defining Types of Illegitimacy

Davis has also outlined the major structural forms of illegitimacy—that is, the five rules of childbirth, which, if violated, make the child illegitimate. The first rule is that the child should be born *after* a marriage. The union may be one of many promiscuous relations, or may instead be that of an engaged couple. The second rule forbids adulterous procreation. In such a case of illegitimacy, the man may be married, or the woman, or both, thus creating three sub-types of adulterous illegitimacy.

Third, a rule of incest may be violated, and an illegitimate child may be born from the union of mother-son, father-daughter, or brother-sister. Another broad rule forbids childbirth to a man and woman of different castes. Finally, a rule of much narrower application prohibits childbirth to those who are required to be celibate, such as priests.[2]

All these rules together make up nine forms of illegitimacy. Not all are possible in every society. Most have no celibate statuses. In most African societies, the second and third sub-types of adulterous illegitimacy would hardly be possible, because the rules of kinship have been organized to guarantee legitimacy to the child born of a marriage. Children are highly coveted, and inquiry into their biological paternity would be unlikely. The mother might be punished for her adultery, but the social position of the child within his kinship network would be clear. For example, in a matrilineage (a descent grouping reckoning ancestry from a known person, through the female line, and acting at times as a collectivity) the child would of course belong to his mother's line.

In some societies castes or caste-like strata exist. The Negro-White division in the U. S. is one type of caste, although the lines are weakening. In India thousands of sub-castes still exist, whose interrelations are defined by myriad rules aimed essentially at preserving ritual purity. These regulations specify, for example, who may hand what kinds of food to whom (thus, a Brahmin is at the peak of caste, and thus can usefully be hired as a cook, since anyone may eat any kind of food from his hands), whose touch is polluting, who may marry whom, and so on. A few sections of sub-castes permit intermarriage with certain others whom they deem acceptable (for example, two sub-groups of Brahmins). This relationship is not equalitarian, since women are defined as marrying "up" the small caste distance to the higher sub-section or sub-caste. However, most crossing of caste lines is forbidden socially, though now permissible by law.

Caste-crossing in marriage or outside it is viewed as highly improper, but of course this disapproval is only a more extreme version of the disapproval that an upper-class family in a rigidly stratified society feels when one of their members marries "downward." This case would not, within the context of this chapter, be viewed as a case of illegitimacy unless the marriage were forbidden by law, by a monarch, or by very strong norms. Those who marry across caste in contemporary India are likely to be outcaste, and those who have an illegiti-

[1] Crane Brinton, *French Revolutionary Legislation on Illegitimacy 1789–1904* (Cambridge: Harvard University Press, 1936), pp. 82–83.
[2] Kingsley Davis, "The Forms of Illegitimacy," *Social Forces* (1939), 18:77–89.

mate inter-caste child are almost certain to be. Where the caste system is flourishing, a legal inter-caste marriage is impossible. Thus any inter-caste child is, as it were, twice illegitimate, since he is born outside marriage and outside caste.

Marriage can "solve" the problem of illegitimacy of only the first of Davis' types—when two unmarried people produce offspring. In all the other forms, the statuses of the individuals forbid marriage as a solution. It is also evident that there is less social disapproval of the first form than of the others. Moreover, disapproval is still less intense if a marriage is *likely* to occur, as would be true of a betrothed couple. These facts suggest that as a next step in analyzing the relation of the family to the society we might consider (1) a wider range of illegitimacy types, and (2) the *degree* of social disapproval. Even the first form mentioned above has a very different meaning in the Caribbean countries, where a high percentage of the population may live together in a consensual union and have children before marriage, or break up the union without marrying. Most of the countries in that region have illegitimacy rates of 30 per cent or more, and in several (e.g., Grenada, Jamaica, the Dominican Republic) the rate is over 60 per cent. Obviously, if a large segment or a majority of the population begin their lives as illegitimates, this status cannot carry so great a stigma as in our own society, where the rate is about 5 per cent.

Similarly, in a period of social disorganization, such as during a protracted revolution, social controls may weaken. Then the rate of illegitimacy may rise, and social disapproval will diminish. The *forms* of illegitimacy would be the same, but their social meaning would be different. In a society with clear lines of demarcation between classes and with strong barriers against social mobility, as in seventeenth-century France, a nobleman might have children by his mistress. Only rarely were such fathers able or willing to obtain noble rank for their illegitimate offspring, but neither did these offspring necessarily take a lowly position in the society. Their fathers could and sometimes did protect and help them.

These examples suggest that although illegitimacy can be defined *legally* and formally, in fact the various types make up a range of *socially* very different patterns, under different intensities of social disapproval, and with very different consequences for the social structure as well as for the individuals concerned. The following list is at present only speculative, and is arranged by the increasing degree of likely social disapproval. The ordering also follows roughly the degree of apparent disruption in the social structure caused by the illegitimacy. As you will notice, however, even this tentative ranking will have to be qualified by empirical research, especially directed toward ascertaining *who* or *which* classes disapprove less of each type of illegitimacy.

Types of Illegitimacy

1. Consensual union
2. Concubinage where it is institutionalized (traditional China and Japan)
3. Lower-class illegitimacy
4. Liaison of nobleman with mistress in pre-industrial Western society
5. Childbirth during betrothal
6. Casual relationship, followed by marriage
7. Adulterous, only the man being married
8. Union of a person in a celibate status with either another celibate or a non-celibate
9. Adulterous, only the woman being married
10. Adulterous, both parties being married
11. Union of upper-caste woman with lower-caste man
12. Incestuous, brother-sister
13. Incestuous, father-daughter
14. Incestuous, mother-son

23

Although empirical research is needed to ascertain whether this frankly speculative ranking is correct, the list affords a basis for several further steps in the analysis of illegitimacy. First, a birth can be *legally* classed as illegitimate or not, but *socially* there are many gradations or degrees of deviation from full social acceptance. Second, the child and mother are not usually killed, and so have to be placed *some*where, under varying degrees of disapproval. Further research is needed to learn just what happens to them in various societies.

Perhaps more important is that the disapproval seems to be correlated roughly with the amount of disruption created by the illegitimacy, but disapproval also varies, depending both on who the offending parties are and who judges them. The upper social strata do not disapprove much of the illegitimacy occurring among the lower classes, but disapprove intensely if one of the offending parties is an upper-class woman, and still more strongly if her liaison is with a lower-class man. By contrast, in the last instance, no doubt lower-class men would feel little moral disapproval of *him* (but some envy), and considerable disapproval of *her*.

The most intense disapproval is directed against incestuous illegitimacy. First of all, it violates the incest taboos found universally in every society, according to which sexual relations are forbidden among members of the nuclear family except for husband and wife. These rules have several results or functions. They force the young in each generation to leave the nuclear family in order to find mates. Thereby, the society is made more cohesive, for many links are forged between families that might otherwise turn inward on themselves. The idiosyncrasies or innovations of a given family are ironed out or distributed more widely within the family. Sexual competition is eliminated from the nuclear family, which might otherwise split it open. Thus, we see again that rules of legitimacy are central in the relations of the family with the larger social structure.

A child of an incestuous union creates a special problem of social placement, because its status is so confused, as is that of its parents. If the child is born to a union between daughter and father, then its mother is also its sister. Its father is married to its grandmother, and its father is simultaneously its grandfather. Its brother (half-brother) is also its uncle (i.e., the brother of its mother). Similar status discrepancies arise if the child is the offspring of a brother-sister union, or a mother-son union. Obviously a marriage will not "solve" these problems, but only exacerbate them. Such marriages are forbidden, and in any event would not iron out the status discrepancies of the family members.

If a central element in understanding illegitimacy is the placement of the child, it follows that lower-caste or lower-class illegitimacy is of less concern to the society than is illegitimacy in other social strata. Lineage and family honor are much less a focus of attention in the lower social strata. There is usually no property to inherit, and thus none to protect by making certain that the proper families are united. The families of the young man and woman lose less rank if an illegitimate child is born. Moreover, lower-strata families control their young less strictly than do the upper. One consequence is that the illegitimacy rate is higher toward the lower social strata.

Although, of course, the class position of the parents is not recorded on a child's birth certificate, indirect evidence in all countries supports this conclusion, i.e., an inverse correlation between class and illegitimacy rate. In the U.S., for example, 44 per cent of illegitimate children in 1958 were either living in adoptive homes of some kind, or were receiving help from the federal Aid to Dependent Children program. For White children this figure was 79 per cent. Illegitimacy by "color" leads to a similar conclusion, since Negroes are on the average poorer than Whites. In 1957 it was estimated that about 2 per cent of White births were illegitimate, as against 21 per cent of Negro births. Ninety-seven per cent of U.S. parents of legitimate children could afford in 1955 to pay for a physician when their children were born; for parents of illegitimate children the figure was 82 per cent, and, of course, payment was often made by a social-work agency. In several southern states, 40 to 50 per cent of illegitimate Negro children were born without a physician in attendance. Mothers of illegitimate children in urban areas are more likely to come from areas of low income.

An illegitimate birth is more scandalous in the upper or middle social strata; so much that more effort is expended to hide the fact when it occurs. Middle-class girls in the U.S. are more likely to travel far away from their homes to bear their children, and to turn over the child to an adoption agency. Pressure on a couple to marry is also heavier in these strata. With sufficient foresight and money, none of the girl's friends need know that she was even pregnant, and her absence can simply be explained as a trip to visit relatives. Economically advantaged families can even avoid an illegitimate birth altogether, by paying for an abortion. For these reasons, not only is the illegitimacy rate higher toward the lower social strata but there the illegitimate birth is socially more conspicuous.

This class difference means that illegitimate children are likely to experience a higher disease and death rate, to receive less adequate education, and to obtain less satisfactory jobs. They are also more likely themselves to produce illegitimate children when they become adults.

The disadvantages suffered by the illegitimate child are a combination of the legal stipulations concerning illegitimacy, its probable class position, the lack of adequate parental care, and the social customs that are social obstacles to opportunity. The laws adopted early in this country aimed at preventing the child from becoming a charge on the state, and placed primary obligation on the mother. Only in this century has legislation been directed at seeking to establish paternity and at forcing this responsibility on the father. New laws, as yet not passed in a majority of states, have removed the fact of illegitimacy from the birth record. In recent times the child has acquired the right to inherit from his mother. (Since his tie with the father is unknown officially, or vague, or narrowly limited, the child does not inherit from the father.) Modern social legislation now attempts increasingly to protect both mother and child.

At the same time, it is an illusion to suppose that by some combination of liberal social-welfare laws the child will somehow be given a position equal to that of the legitimate child. Laws aimed at protecting the illegitimate simply underscore the social and legal fact that his position *is* different. As long as social customs dictate the terms of an appropriate marriage, the child born outside those limits will suffer some stigma and disadvantages.

These problems will vary with the type of illegitimacy. The situation of such a child must be weighed by comparing his position to that of a legitimate child of the same class. The child born of a consensual union in Jamaica, for example, will suffer few disadvantages compared with his playmates. Most of them either are or were illegitimate, and their lot is little worse than that of youngsters born of equally poor but married parents.

By contrast, an illegitimate child born to a U.S. middle-class couple suffers far more disadvantage if he is born to an unmarried middle-class couple, for it will have few or none of the benefits of that class position, unless of course it is adopted by middle-class parents. However, the problem of comparison is more difficult in a cross-caste or cross-class union. The child is usually the responsibility of the mother, who is likely to be lower class, and thus it will be a member of the lower social stratum. In the U.S., a child of a cross-caste union —i.e., Negro and White—will be treated as a Negro. He may suffer only a few disadvantages compared to other Negroes of his economic position, but his position will be much less favorable than his father's is.

Historically, of course, there are many instances in which the illegitimate child of a cross-class or cross-caste union received support and protection from the upper-class father, and thus the position of both mother and child were better than others in the lower social stratum. Again, however, they did not have the still greater advantages that a legitimate union would have given them; but in any event a legal union between castes is not possible. In the American Old South, death for the male was the social penalty for a cross-caste sexual union in which the male was lower caste, if his identity was discovered. In India the same result was likely, along with the deaths of mother and child. If not put to death, mother and child would be outcastes.

The Control of Illegitimacy

As in other areas of possible deviant behavior, most people are not kept from illegitimacy only by fear of its consequences, but by (1) internal controls, which make the individual feel it is morally wrong to run the risk, and (2) social controls that warn the individual long before any intimacy occurs. Friends and kin caution the girl, and sometimes the young man as well. The girl is surrounded by a network of people who set the conditions for her interaction with the young man, can bear witness that they were indeed together, and may pressure the young man later to marry the girl. The couple is alone on a date, but not before or after, so that the situation is not anonymous.

In the past, the Western upper and middle classes have used a *duenna* or chaperone system to prevent all adult males (except perhaps close kin or respected old men) from ever being alone with an unmarried nubile girl. Because the focus of attention was premarital illegitimacy more than adultery, the married woman was given more freedom, and indeed marriage was viewed as one way by which a young girl might obtain release from at least some of these burdensome restrictions. Of course adultery was likely to cause trouble, but the married woman had responsibilities of her own, and was an adult, so that she could move about more freely. With the marriage settled, it has been assumed any child of a married woman was legitimate, unless clear proof of the contrary was possible.

Lower-class families could not afford the cost of a special person to guard their unmarried women, but though lower-class women have generally enjoyed more freedom than upper-class women, they were likely to be jealously watched. In some of the less urbanized regions of the West, such as rural Greece, Sicily and southern Italy, and rural Spain, this jealous guardianship still persists.

The Puritans of the seventeenth century emphasized strong moral repression, defining any extramarital sexual behavior as sinful. To be sure, they also watched their women carefully.

In most primitive societies, premarital sexual intercourse has been permitted. Under such conditions of high risk, a combination of factors has kept the illegitimacy rate low. First, menstruation typically occurs later than in Western societies. In the U.S. the average is between 12 and 13 years, as against 14 to 16 years in nonliterate societies for which data are available. Second, present evidence suggests that for a period varying from 1 to 3 years after menstrua-

legitimacy and illegitimacy

tion, the young girl is relatively infertile, so that in societies where adolescents engage in sexual relations she may run little risk of pregnancy. Finally, marriage takes place early, and is still earlier if the girl becomes pregnant. Consequently, the illegitimacy rate is likely to be low.

In the U.S., it is likely that pregnancy precedes one-fourth or more of all marriages. This fact, in a country where constraceptives are available and widely used, suggests a very high rate of premarital sexual intercourse. On the other hand, a high (but unknown) percentage of those who become pregnant are emotionally attached to one another, and most either make a final decision to marry, or move ahead the date of the intended marriage. Indeed, the *peak* month of marriage for those who marry *after* conception is *2 months* after conception. Since about 6 weeks must pass before a laboratory test can prove that a woman is pregnant, the evidence of haste seems clear, and points up how strong are the social pressures bearing on the couple.

Although doubtless the percentage of the U.S. population who engage in premarital intercourse has increased over the past generation, it is likely that the slight apparent increase in the illegitimacy rate (from about 4' per cent to nearly 5 per cent) is due more to improvements in birth-recording procedures than to any change in social pattern. In most Western nations, there has been either a slight drop, or no change, over the past half-century. Scattered evidence suggests that premarital conception with a modest or low rate of illegitimacy has been widespread in the West for centuries. In one French area a check of marriages and first births (using parish registers) found that about 30 per cent of the marriages of workers and artisans were preceded by conception in the late eighteenth century.

Although lay opinion tends to suppose that sexual morals have been deteriorating, and that rural people are more moral than urban people, the evidence is at best unclear. The supposed high level of "rural morality" may be only a widespread myth. In much of north and central Europe, and in rural regions of France, Holland, and even Scotland, a widespread pattern of courtship during the eighteenth century included premarital sexual intercourse and, especially in south Germany, Austria, and Sweden, a relatively high rate of illegitimacy (about 20 per cent). Outsiders were barred from this courtship pattern, since they were of a different social status and could not be held to account. The pairing-off process was evaluated and shaped by peers as well as parents. Young men could not escape their responsibilities without leaving the region and thus abandoning their sole means of livelihood, the family farm. Marriage often post-dated the birth of a child, but the couple was eventually united legally. Both church and state denounced the pattern, but in some regions it continued until well into the nineteenth century. It permitted some sexual freedom among the young, but maintained close social control over marriage. This pattern also existed in rural Japan until after the Meiji Restoration of 1868. These practices have gradually dissolved, so that in such areas the formal rate of illegitimacy has decreased (i.e., the percentage born out of wedlock). It must be kept in mind, however, that under the older system social controls were strong, and almost every young mother did marry the father of her child eventually, and with the approval of both parents. Consequently, the social placement and care of the child was certain. There was a sociological father and, not long after the birth of the child, a legal one as well. Thus, under the old system the rate of *social* illegitimacy was low.

A very different pattern is found in the New World, from the southern United States to the tip of South America, and including the Caribbean. This pattern shows how closely linked is illegitimacy with the integration of the society.

27

Particular provinces in some New-World countries have illegitimacy rates of 80 per cent or more. A small group of mainland countries have rates higher than 70 per cent, and most of the political units in the New World have rates over 30 per cent. Among non-Whites in the southern U.S., rates between 20 and 30 per cent were recorded in 1957. A few of these rates are given below.

Illegitimacy Rates in Selected New-World Countries *

Country	Rate	Year
Chile	16%	1958
Mexico	22.5	1956
Costa Rica	25	1957
Colombia	28	1957
Peru	43	1955
Martinique	48	1956
Venezuela	57	1955
Honduras	65	1957
Guatemala	70	1957
Panama	71	1956

* Data from *United Nations Demographic Year Book Questionnaire*. This section is adapted from my "Illegitimacy, Anomie, and Cultural Penetration," *American Sociological Review* (December 1961), 26:910–925.

Such high rates might suggest that the Principle of Legitimacy is incorrect and should be abandoned. However, the Principle asserts only that every society has such a standard, a rule of legitimacy, not that everyone obeys it. After all, no moral rule is obeyed by everyone. Nevertheless, if so high a percentage of the population pay little attention to it, then perhaps they do not believe in it either. If they do not accept it as a *value*, then Malinowski was wrong.

It has been maintained that the high rates are simply the remnants of "native customs," survivals of social patterns that once were common among the original inhabitants of the New World. This explanation must be discarded. Many studies of New-World Indian tribes have been made, and they show that no such tolerance of illegitimacy ever existed, so that the modern pattern cannot be such a "remnant." In the Caribbean and in the U.S. South, the population came from African tribes where childbirth outside of marriage was disapproved, so that again these high rates could not have come from older African customs. Moreover, among these societies from which the populations of New-World countries stemmed, a wide range of kinship patterns existed: low and high divorce rates, patriliny and matriliny, polygyny and monogamy. But illegitimacy rates have been *generally* high among these New-World populations. That is, the hundreds of family systems and societies from which the ancestors of these people came were so varied that they would not have shared so peculiar a modern trait, high illegitimacy rates. We must therefore look for another explanation.

Another frequent explanation is that a "new subculture" has developed in the New World, in which the consensual union is the "moral equivalent" of a legal marriage, supported by the community as fully as a marriage, and giving the child exactly the same status as that of a child born to a legal union. This explanation is used to support ethnic or racial stereotypes, according to which

28

people in the lowest social class live a happy-go-lucky life, sexually free and irresponsible, and content in their poverty. However, wherever researchers have not been satisfied to report only the behavioral fact of illegitimacy and have probed into values and attitudes (i.e., their ideals, aspirations, and evaluations) as shown by both words and deeds, it becomes clear that mother and child have a lower status outside the legal union, that women prefer to be married, and that children may push their parents to marry legally. Even where the illegitimacy rate is high, a majority of people eventually do marry. Clearly, people would not do so, if it were true that the consensual union were as highly evaluated as the legal union.

In the lower classes of most New-World countries, and including a substantial part of the southern U.S. Negro population, young girls are likely to enter their first sexual experiences or a consensual union without support from kin or peer groups to aid them in the bargaining process of courtship. A few girls, with unusual beauty, a strong kinship network, or a bit of property, may marry legally in their first union. In most other societies of the world, on the other hand, the marriageable girl has this support of kin and peers in the bargaining process whether or not she has outstanding qualities or endowments. Here, then, we have an interesting anomaly. How did so great a discrepancy develop between the ideal and actual behavior?

The European conquest of the New World was not merely political and military, as it was in India, Indonesia, or Egypt, or as was the Manchu conquest of China in the seventeenth century. It was also a *social and cultural conquest*. Although the inhabitants of Latin-American countries look like their ancestors of several centuries ago, most of their cultural patterns are Western, not Indian. Popular accounts of experiences in the Caribbean islands emphasize such esoteric items as voodoo, drumbeats in the jungle night, and women carrying bundles on their heads, but the cultural patterns are overwhelmingly Western, not African. The lower classes of Jamaica do not speak Cockney English, but their language is now an English dialect. In the New World, except for a few tribal pockets, the older cultural patterns have been penetrated and undermined, and though aboriginal traits remain (e.g., the use of okra as a food, the sacredness of an ancient god here and there) most inhabitants of the New World must be counted as participants in one variant or another of the Western culture complex.

Two main types of massive influence created this result. One was characteristic of the southern U.S. and the Caribbean, a physical destruction of most of the native inhabitants, and a substitution of alien slaves from Africa. These were mixed geographically by design, to prevent them from maintaining their African social systems or communities, and thus they could not maintain their African cultural heritage. Their descendents were emancipated late in the nineteenth century, and later generations occupy the bottom social strata in these countries. Some individuals have moved to higher social positions as well.

The other main type of cultural penetration was socially more complex and took place on the mainland, from Mexico to the tip of South America. After the conquest of the three great population centers, where the Iberians sought gold, they extended their control to other regions where the exploitation of labor offered the chance of riches. They nearly defeated their own economic aims in the late sixteenth and early seventeenth centuries, since from one-third to one-half of their subjects died from the diseases they introduced, and from overwork and undernourishment. Many native communities were left intact for a while, and native rulers were permitted to rule in some communities, so that the social structures remained intact; but after 1600 this rul-

29

ing stratum was generally removed. The Church was backed by force in its efforts to convert, so that the native religions lost their integrative influence. In addition, the Iberians transplanted large segments of the native populations to facilitate political administration, a further factor in reducing the strength of the traditional social systems. A caste system developed which relegated the natives to the bottom of the social ladder and made any upward mobility difficult. For nearly 300 years after the initial invasions and plundering there was little economic expansion, so that the rulers did not need to train their subjects or to permit them to occupy high social positions.

Thus, after the period of conquest, the Indians and Negroes could not adequately socialize their young to believe strongly in their own traditional values, since the political, economic, and other social forces were imposed and maintained by the Iberian conquerors. The natives came to accept the superiority of Iberian values through religious conversion, adjustment to political domination, and the failure of their own social systems to support the alternative, traditional ideas. On the other hand, the establishment of a caste system forbade the usual reward for full cultural assimilation and high social mobility. In this respect, the process was different from the cultural assimilation of immigrants in U.S. cities in the late-nineteenth and early-twentieth centuries.

The slavery systems in the U.S. and the Caribbean exhibit similar processes, although in this great region no towns, villages, or societies (except those made up of slaves who escaped) made up of descendents of a single tribe were permitted. Consequently, for many generations the majority of these populations lived in *cultures* that were not internally integrated, or integrated fully with the dominant culture of the rulers, and in *social systems* that were not internally integrated socially, or fully integrated with the dominant social systems of the rulers.

It is the *community*, not the individual or the family, that can maintain conformity to the norm of legitimacy, by giving or withholding prestige and honor. The individual can risk illegitimacy or not, but there will be little loss of honor if the community grants almost as much respect for marriage as for non-marriage. Unless it is integrated culturally and socially, the community cannot easily punish the deviant, and indeed will care little about the deviation. High individual or family conformity to a given norm depends on both the community commitment to the *value* itself, and to the strength of its *social controls*. The conditions in the New World from the U.S. Negro South to Tierra del Fuego created a high rate of illegitimacy, since it weakened both the norms and the social controls.

legitimacy and illegitimacy

mate selection
and marriage
four

The preceding chapters have shown the utility of viewing the family not merely as a relationship between husband and wife, or parents and children, but also as a set of links between the social network of family members and the larger network of the society. In analyzing family systems we look not only at the social relations internal to a given family, but also between family and society.

Consequently, in considering the processes of courtship and mate selection, we see again that the larger society is interested in the result. Always the two family networks of the marrying couple are thereby linked, and thus still more distant networks are also involved. Both family lines have some rank in the stratification system, whose stability depends in part on who marries whom. Intermarriage is the best index that one family line considers the other approximately equal socially or economically.

Within the families themselves, one gains and the other loses a member. (If the woman moves to the location of her husband's family, the system is called *patrilocal*; if he moves to that of her family, the system is *matrilocal*. Moving to an independent household is called *neolocality*.) Where they reside determines to a large extent the frequency of social interaction with one set of kin as against another. Marriage forges a new social link, and thus added strength; but perhaps also the loss of a productive worker, or a friendly kinsman. In many societies the loss of an adult woman as a bride is compensated for by a "bride price," or by the man working for a period, called "groom service." Entrance into the family of the spouse creates numerous new role obligations, and necessarily some new adjustments and strains.

Consequently, a marriage sets in motion a host of consequences, in which many kinsmen are concerned—not to mention the husband and wife themselves. In all societies, complex rules guide the process of mate selection and eventual marriage. The marriage ceremonial is a ritual of passage for the couple; a young man and woman pass ritually into adult status with its new rights and responsibilities. It also announces the society's approval of the union. Thereby the kinship network accepts new role obligations. In Western nations, the state has for centuries played a larger part in marriage law than in most nations of the East, but marriage is a public matter in all societies, since the larger society has a stake in its consequences.

The ceremony of marriage itself is highly visible, but more than that it is a symbol of the culmination of many processes that are subtle and important. Indeed, many who marry see only the choice of their spouse as the real decison. In the U.S., for example, people "date" with the understanding that a date, or even many dates, need not mean a serious commitment, and need not require any explicit decision about the meaning of the relationship. On the other hand, a closer look at the process of courtship and marriage choice will disclose that many *implicit* decisions, choices, or alternatives are being followed, and that these shape or determine the final choice of the marital partner.

The Market Structure of Marriage

Fundamentally, the process of mate selection functions like a market system. This system varies from one society to another, with respect to who controls the transactions, what are the rules of exchange, and the relative evaluation of various qualities. In the upper-class Japanese and Chinese societies of the past, these transactions were controlled by the elders —formally, legally, and publicly by the men, though elder women often made the real decision. According to the rules of traditional Arab societies, a man's family paid a bride price for the woman, while in the Brahmin castes of India her family paid a groom price. The rules may also require counter-gifts of some kind. As to the evaluation of different qualities, the honor of the family line may count for more than the individual traits of the marrying couple, or the beauty of a woman may be as valuable as a man's wealth.

Of course, the participants in this process may not *think* of themselves as "driving a bargain." Parents may instead see themselves as "seeking the best for their children"; or a young man may see himself as seeking the hand of his beloved. Many do not even consider some of the factors that clearly affect the final choice. To understand this process better, we can begin with our own system of courtship and mate choice. It is *formally* free, and legally almost any man *can* marry almost any woman. On the other hand, the patterns of choice show clearly that the number of eligibles is in fact highly restricted. Moreover, even though the vocabulary of love is used widely in this country, almost everyone does at times use the language of bargaining. Let us begin with the familiar pattern of dating in the U.S. As Winch points out, it has several important functions, or consequences. First, it is a popular form of recreation, and thus an end in itself. Neither of the two persons incurs any

mate selection and marriage

obligation to continue dating after the first experience.[1] Second, it is part of the socialization experience, especially in acquainting individuals with the mysteries of the opposite sex. Thereby, third, the individual explores his own personality and tests his powers in the dating situation. Dating eventually culminates in the selection of a mate, its central function for our present purposes. Finally, it emphasizes the pattern of stratification in the society. Indeed, the last two are closely bound. If dating were only recreation and had nothing to do with marriage, class elements might not be so important in adolescent dating.

Bargaining and Homogamy

Before looking at concrete findings, let us emphasize that all mate-selection systems press toward *homogamous* marriages as a result of the bargaining process. That is, in general, "like marries like"—with reference to a wide variety of traits. If the girl comes from a wealthy family, her family associates with other wealthy families, and by her wealth she can command a good "price" in the marriage market. That is, other wealthy families will find her an acceptable bride for their sons. Similarly, if her family is high in prestige or power, other families at that level will consider her acceptable, and her family need not ally itself with lower-ranking families in order to find an acceptable groom. The untalented, homely, poor man may *aspire* to a bride with highly desirable qualities, but he cannot offer enough to induce either her or her family to choose him, for they can find a groom with more highly valued qualities.

Thus, the process of seeking a bride with highly ranked traits usually leads to finding a spouse with traits at about the level of the potential groom. The same processes operate, of course, in the dating patterns of Western countries. Homogamy is supported by various rules of *endogamy*, and is achieved against some rules of *exogamy*. Endogamy simply means marrying within the group, such as a religious faith, a caste, or a nation. Exogamy requires, instead, marrying outside certain groupings. All societies have both kinds of rules, but they obviously refer to different *groups*. Incest taboos are rules of exogamy, and so are rules requiring an individual to marry outside the clan. The weight of class factors in dating is striking, in spite of the fact that some part of adolescent "rebellion" is directed against adult "materialism" and in favor of social relationships based on the whole personality, on human qualities. In one study of high-school dating, 61 per cent of all "dates" belonged in the same class and 35 per cent in an adjacent class. When a boy crossed class lines (using a 5-class breakdown), in 2 out of 3 times he dated a girl in a lower class; if a girl crossed the lines, in 2 out of 3 cases she dated upward.[2] Moreover, and of equal importance for an understanding of this process, those who dated in a *higher* class were likely to have *special qualities:* the girls were popular or pretty; the boys were outstanding athletes, or high-school leaders. That is, they were able to gain the advantage of dating with a person in a higher class position by offering in exchange another valued trait. Even in this early phase of courtship, then, we see a pattern of bargaining and class influence.

Other qualities as well must be included in our perspective on bargaining and homogamy. Dating, for instance is also more likely to occur between

---

[1] Robert F. Winch, "The Functions of Dating in Middle-Class America," in Winch, Robert McGinnis, and Herbert R. Barringer (eds.), *Selected Studies in Marriage and the Family* (New York: Holt, Rinehart and Winston, 1962), pp. 506–509.
[2] August B. Hollingshead, *Elmtown's Youth* (New York: Wiley, 1949), pp. 230–232.

high-school students of the same *school* class.[3] In Hollingshead's sample, half of the dates took place between students in the same school class (i.e., freshman dated freshman, and so on). One-third of the boys' dates were with girls a class below them in the school; and one-third of girls' dates were with boys one school class higher than they. Since it is usually the boy who dates the younger girl, the senior girl is sometimes embarrassed by being dateless. Consequently, in 62 per cent of the cases in which a girl dates a younger boy, it is a senior girl who dates a junior boy.

Of course, this pattern is also to be found in the dating that precedes marriage, for in general those who marry are close to one another in age. In 1959 the median age of brides married for the first time to grooms also never before married was 19.9 years. The age of these grooms was 22.4 years. Of marriages of this type in the marriage registration area, 16 per cent were entered into by males 21 years of age (this may be a slight exaggeration, since this is the legal age for males in many states, and some falsify their ages in order to marry). Three-fourths of these men married young women 18 to 21 years of age. When the groom is older, the age of the bride does not increase parallel to that of the groom, but lags behind somewhat.

Studies made in the U.S. over the past generation also show that people who marry are likely to live close to one another. About half of urban marriages occur between men and women who live approximately 1 mile from one another, or 14 city blocks. About one-fourth of the couples live within 3 blocks of one another. Residential propinquity is usually indicative of class similarity, since those who live close to one another are also more likely to be of the same class. A closer examination of the facts shows that class is also a differentiating variable, since those from middle- or upper-occupational groups are more likely to travel greater distances in seeking their spouses. In one Ohio sample, the median distance traveled by the unskilled for their spouses was less than 5 blocks.[4]

This suggestion that Cupid's wings do not travel far in any one flight should not be explained only by class. Propinquity is a little-noticed but powerful factor in the development of social relations. Its social importance is that it increases or decreases the likelihood of unplanned, chance social encounters between strangers or acquaintances, thus affording them less opportunity for easy social interaction. If people have traits that might attract them to one another, propinquity increases the possibility that they will find this out. People who live close together are more likely to attend the same schools, shop in the same stores, travel the same buses, or simply greet one another on the street as familiar strangers. A considerable but unmeasured part of our social interaction is shaped by this apparently spatial factor. In addition, space also has a time and energy meaning. A boy who is deeply in love may be willing to travel an hour to take his sweetheart home several nights a week, but a boy is also less likely to fall in love with such a girl to begin with, since he may not go to the trouble of exposing himself to her charms long enough to become intensely attached. Distance may not increase his reluctance as much, of course, if travel is only a small drain on his financial and energy resources. Indeed, one reason why men at the upper occupational levels travel farther in their courtships is that they can more easily afford the greater cost in transportation and communication.

If the reader mentally lists the marriages among the people he knows, he

[3] *Ibid.*, pp. 225–226.
[4] Marin R. Koller, "Residential and Occupational Propinquity," in Winch, McGinnis, and Barringer, *Selected Studies in Marriage and the Family*, p. 476.

mate selection and marriage

will very likely learn what most studies show, that brides and grooms tend to find one another within their own social class. The exact percentage of intra-class marriages depends on the number of classes used (if 6 to 8 classes are used instead of 3, the number of *cross*-class marriages will be greater), and also on the index of class used (education, income, occupation, etc.). If only 3 classes are used, based primarily on occupation, slightly more than half of the marriages are between men and women in the same class. In Hollingshead's study of New Haven marriages, using six classes, both partners came from the same class of residential area in 58 per cent of the unions. Eighty-three per cent came from the same *or* adjacent classes.[5] When women marry into a different class, they are more likely to marry upward in class, or *hypergamously*.

Most marriages are homogamous with respect to race. Negro-White marriages are rare in the U.S., though they are very likely increasing. These cross-caste unions deserve special attention in analyzing marriage practices, and will be discussed later in this chapter.

Religious barriers also divide people into smaller pools of homogamous eligibles. Most Protestants accept other Protestants as maritally eligible, with rather little regard for the theological differences among sects. The three great groups, then, are Protestants, Jews, and Catholics. Most marriages occur endogamously within each of them. Jews are most likely to marry endogamously, Catholics next, and Protestants least. Nationwide data on such points are estimates. Very likely over 80 per cent of Jews marry endogamously. In studies done in New Haven, the figure for Catholics was 80 to 90 per cent, but the figure varies with the percentage of Catholics in a given area. In the Southeastern U.S., where the percentage is low (4 to 5%), about half of the marriages of Catholics are interfaith. In the New England states the percentage of interfaith marriages drops to less than one-fourth.

This last fact illustrates a *general* relationship in homogamy: A group is less likely to maintain its barriers against out-marriage if it is small, but a group can remain exclusive if it is large. That is, within a larger group of eligibles the individual can find a potential spouse—i.e., a person who is like himself in being a member of the group, *and* is also similar with respect to wealth, education and so on.

Clearly, these factors include the processes of *both* exclusion and inclusion, and work in opposite directions. Members of a small group have a greater motivation to allow out-marriage because of a shortage of eligibles. But in the same area the members of a larger group would *correspondingly* have *less* reason to leave their own group.

The exact outcome depends on other factors as well, such as the amount of in-group solidarity, the social rank of the group, the effectiveness of its match-making processes, and so on. Catholics in West Texas are less likely to be able to marry Protestants than Catholics in New Mexico, because people of Mexican background (who make up most Catholics in both regions) have a lower social rank in West Texas than in New Mexico. Protestant families are less likely to object to a prospective *German* Catholic bride than to an *Italian* Catholic. Jews and Orthordox Greeks are more solidary than Protestants, and also match-make more actively. However, the general outcome is clear, for in both the U.S. and Canada there is an *inverse* relationship between the percentage of the population in a given religious group in the various territories and regions, and the percentage of interfaith marriages. Out-marriages increase as the percentage of the population in each group decreases.

[5] Winch, McGinnis, and Barringer, *Selected Studies in Marriage and the Family*, pp. 485–486.

Religious endogamy in the U.S. masks, as suggested above, the effect of many other social factors. It is doubtful that many marriages are opposed merely because the potential spouse holds different *theological* beliefs. Few Americans even know what these beliefs are, or feel strongly about them. It is the social background, *correlated* with religion, that is weighed. Jewish families will ordinarily have no objection to a young man who never visits the synagogue, if he is at least nominally Jewish. The objections of Protestant families to their children marrying Catholics is as often an objection to a union with a different ethnic group as to church affiliation. Catholics in the U.S. are likely to be identified with ethnic groups whose prestige rating is low: Italians, Mexicans, Puerto Ricans, French-Canadians, Irish in some areas, and Poles or other Central Europeans. In addition, Protestants object to the imperialism implicit in the Catholic Church's insistence that the children of a cross-faith marriage be reared as Catholics.

The complexities of social factors that influence the rate of intrafaith marriages are therefore great, and are not to be explained even primarily by church beliefs. What is significant is that most partners find their spouses within the same large religious group, and that those who attempt to cross the boundaries will face opposition from their friends and family, which may in part be answered by asserting the special virtues of the future spouse. One consequence is that those who cross these barriers are more likely to be less-convinced believers in the church to which they ostensibly belong.

The pattern of homogamy extends also to marital status. Most who marry are of course single, but within each pool the widowed, widowered, and the divorced also marry in a higher proportion than could be attributable to chance.

Well over 100 studies have shown that husband and wife are more alike in a wide range of traits than could be accounted for by chance. It seems clear, however, that young men and women do not spend much thought on whether their date or fiancée possesses similar traits. Rather, homogamy is for the most part the product of other social processes, notably (1) the differential association of people in groups that are more or less homogeneous, and (2) the process of finding one's own level in the courtship market. The first of these makes it less likely that a young man will meet many young women on an informal basis who do *not* share any of his social traits, such as religious class, education, ethnic background, and so on. In addition, if he shows undue attachment to a young woman of a very different background, his family and friends are likely to express some disapproval of his choice.

The second of these processes also leads to homogamy, as noted earlier. The young man might prefer to marry a beautiful, rich girl, and possibly his family would not object; but without outstanding qualities he is not likely to win her from her circle of friends who can at least offer comparable wealth. Her family would oppose a marriage "beneath" her, and her friends would ask what "she sees in him." When one fiancée is seen as being able to command a better match, both kin and friends analyze or criticize the intended union in market terms. The poor talented student is advised to marry late, for example, because after his abilities have been proved he can make a more advantageous match. Moreover, contrary to the folklore of America, those who *are* engaged also evaluate the merits of their beloved, and compare their alternative marital chances. Homogamy results, then, from the slow sifting of individuals into pairs whose traits are more or less equally valued in the current marriage market. The value system, however, does not rate all traits equally, nor all equally in the two sexes. The ability to swim with speed and grace or to dance well has

mate selection and marriage

less value, for example, than family prestige. When a woman's beauty enables her to marry above her class, there is some grumbling among the eligible women in her husband's circle, and some envy among those in her own, but the marriage is viewed as an appropriate exchange (not necessarily as a *wise* exchange). On the other hand, the rich woman who marries a lower-class man for his handsomeness is laughed at, and he is classified, even if erroneously, as a variety of gigolo or fortune hunter. Beauty and charm are thought of as intrinsically part of the female social position, and properly to be used in the market. Talent in one's occupation is a corresponding attribute in a man.

This difference can be seen in a striking form in one type of extreme heterogamy, Negro-White marriages. Caste rules, and in some states caste laws, forbid such marriages. Almost everyone believes that they will fail, and at best will be tragedies for the resulting children, although no appropriate studies have been made.

When such marriages do occur, they are mainly hypogamous. That is, in the various compilations of the few data available, it is the White woman who marries into the *lower* caste, from 3 to 10 times as frequently as the White man marries into the lower caste. A closer examination of the exchange of advantages in cross-caste marriages suggests that they are primarily of two types. In one, *both* parties have repudiated the caste system ideologically, and both hold relatively advantageous class positions. That is, they are in different castes, but in the same class, usually middle class or higher. In this type of marriage neither males nor females are more likely to marry across caste lines. Since both partners deny the relevance of caste in the exchange, it does not make the female more willing than the male to marry cross-caste.

The more common union, however, involves a middle- or upper-class Negro man with a lower- or lower middle-class White woman. Merton has analyzed theoretically the likelihood of various types of cross-caste marriage, and points out that this type permits the male to trade his *class* advantage as a provider for his wife's advantage in *caste* position.[6] A lower-class White male could not so easily make a similar exchange with a wealthy Negro woman, because this would deny his role as provider. And, of course, the union between the White man of any class position and a Negro woman in the lower class would likely not issue in marriage, would simply remain a liaison. Both the caste position and his sex permit him to take the initiative in such a union. However, there is no social pressure on him to marry her. Thus, when cross-caste marriages occur, in the U.S., they are likely to be caste-hypogamous. The woman marries into the lower caste, but to an occupationally successful male.

Love as a Factor in Marriage

Love is viewed as a threat to the stratification system in many societies, and elders warn against using love as the basis for mate selection. However, it is clear that if the sober factors of wealth, occupation, caste, age, or religion do not *substitute* for love, they nevertheless create the framework within which it operates. Since the marriageable population of the U.S. is gradually segregated into pools of eligibles with similar social backgrounds, relatively free dating patterns can exist without disrupting the stratification system. In fact, there is *not* a completely free market in courtship or mate selec-

---

[6] Robert K. Merton, "Intermarriage and the Social Structure: Fact and Theory," in *Psychiatry* (August 1941), 4:361–374. See also the complementary article by Kingsley Davis, "Intermarriage in Caste Societies," *American Anthropologist* (July–September 1941), 43:376–395.

tion. Rather, as in economic exchanges, there are many smaller markets in which few are eligible to participate. It is within each such market that considerable freedom exists.

Nevertheless, love *is* important in the formation of marriages. Yet only in the West, and only recently, has love come to be viewed as an almost necessary precipitating event that heralds marriage. How love affects the social structure can be interpreted sociologically. Before discussing these consequences, the psychological process of love-choice should be analyzed.

The processes of sifting and association creates pools of eligibles, who have roughly the same value in the marriage market. However, those processes do not explain how the *final* pairing occurs that leads to marriage. The Theory of Complementary Needs offers an explanation for these romantic attachments.

Beginning from Henry A. Murray's conception of psychological needs, Robert F. Winch and his associates have suggested that "in mate-selection each individual seeks within his or her field of eligibles for that person who gives the greatest promise of providing him or her with maximum need gratification." [7] That is, those who fall in love are likely to be *alike* in their social traits, but *complementary* in their psychological needs. One who needs to be helped or nurtured is likely to be attracted by someone who needs to give help. Both will obtain satisfaction, reward, or pleasure in interacting with one another. A person who has a strong need for *achievement* will, according to this theory, seek out someone who has a strong *vicariousness* need—i.e., who gets satisfaction from seeing that another person is gratified. These needs are not *opposites*; an individual may need to help others, yet also need to be helped himself. Winch and his associates developed a list of 12 needs and 3 general psychological traits, and outlined a series of hypotheses about the likelihood that individuals with a given set of needs will be attracted by persons with another set. Thus, autonomy is paired with deference as well as hostility. Abasement is viewed as complementary to autonomy, dominance, hostility, nurturance, and recognition.

Without analyzing each in turn, we may simply repeat the central hypothesis: "In mate-selection the need-pattern of each spouse will be complementary rather than similar to the need-pattern of the other spouse."

This theory does not assert that within any pool of eligibles each person *can* find another who satisfied his needs completely or adequately. It explains only why each person within that pool finds only certain others attractive. The theory does not predict, either, that those who satisfy each other's needs will be happy after they marry. They may have different tastes, and widely divergent conceptions of the role obligations of husband and wife. In-laws may interfere, or one spouse may become an alcoholic.

Social factors may also prevent the effective operation of complementarity by distorting the individual's perception of the other's psychological pattern. In most societies the male is supposed to show achievement, dominance, and autonomy, and a high percentage will do so even if their own psychological makeup is under strain as a consequence. The *behavioral* conformity, however, may keep most people from discovering the psychological discomfort it masks. Consequently, a woman may feel that certain of her needs will be, or are being, satisfied, and learn only after marriage that her husband really would prefer to be dominated, to pay deference, and dislikes being competitive.

In addition, people vary widely in their ability to perceive or intuit the psychological traits of others, and as a result a few people may feel that their

[7] Robert F. Winch, *Mate Selection* (New York: Harper, 1958), pp. 88–89.

mate selection and marriage

mates are satisfying some of their needs, simply because they misperceive what their mates are doing. A clever woman may dominate without letting her husband know it, for example.

Since this theory has not been fully worked out or tested, further complexities in it should be mentioned. Perhaps most important is the *structure* or *profile* of the needs. How much lack in one kind of gratification, nurturance, for instance, can be made up by how much gratification in another, perhaps deference? If both spouses find their needs are met, but with no great intensity, is this a stabler emotional relationship than one in which some needs are satisfied completely, others hardly at all? Does the satisfaction of one need become more important in one society than another, so that the attraction from one kind of complementarity is likely to be greater in one rather than another?

But though this theory has many interesting ramifications and complexities, its importance would be less if falling in love were, as is so often alleged, common only in the United States, where supposedly people court and date in the romantic Hollywood fashion.

The importance of love in the U.S. has been exaggerated in popular accounts, which frequently argue that it is a poor basis for marriage while failing to take account of the extent to which the selection process leads to pairings between persons of similar backgrounds. Nevertheless, compared to others, the marriage system of the U.S. has given love greater prominence. Here, as in all Western societies to some lesser degree, the child is socialized to fall in love. Falling in love is a common topic of family talk, as it is a theme in movies, television and radio programs, and advertising. Children tease one another about it, and adults engage in mock or serious conversations with youngsters about their "sweethearts." It is taken for granted that eventually almost everyone will decide to marry on the basis of a romantic attachment.

The main connections between the element of love and other social structures in the industrialized West are the following: First, the family unit is relatively independent of the larger kinship group, so that husband and wife are free to love each other without serious competition from their kin. In many societies the husband-wife tie is accorded less emotional prominence. Second, the parent-child tie is strong, and falling in love permits the young person to free himself from this attachment in order to enter the independent status of spouse. The U.S. variant of the Western cultural patterns gives considerable freedom to adolescents, thus increasing the likelihood that they will fall in love. And, of course, love may be viewed as a mechanism for filling the gap left by the decline of arranged marriages. Young people who in another marriage system would be pushed into marriage by their elders are motivated to marry because of love.

However, this last proposition may be turned around: In a system of arranged marriages, various social patterns exist to *prevent* love from *disrupting* the arrangements made by the elders. To understand this relationship more clearly, we can think of the world's societies ranked along a continuum or dimension of *institutionalization* of love as an element in the mate-selection process. At one extreme is the U.S., where the individual has to give a good reason for marrying without being in love. ("I am too old for that sort of thing." "I was poor; he was a good man, and rich.") At the other extreme might be placed the upper classes of classical China or Tokugawa Japan, where love was viewed as a tragedy or at best irrelevant to the elders' choice of the individual's mate. In all societies some individuals do fall in love, but in many this behavior is not regarded as part of the ordinary process of mate selection.

Then we can distinguish the few societies, such as all or most Polynesian societies and the industrialized Western nations, where a *romantic complex* is found—i.e., a considerable degree of institutionalization of love—and societies in which most people *do* fall in love during the courtship period, although the process is not viewed as an *ideological* prescription.

Love is a potential threat to the stratification system, and is controlled in one of several ways. It can disrupt the elders' plans to unite two lineages or family inheritances, or link a high-ranking family with one of low rank to the embarrassment of the former. Property, power, lineage honor, totemic relationships, and other family elements in all societies are believed to flow from one generation to the next through the kinship lines, linked by marriage. Mate choice thus has many consequences. People who fall in love have braved storms of anger, violence, ostracism, and their own fears to be married. To avoid this, mate choice is frequently controlled, so that it is not left to the whim of youngsters.

The fullest possible control can be obtained, naturally, by arranging matters before love can appear. The reader is familiar with one such system, the apparently free courtship system of the U.S., which in fact permits freedom only within somewhat narrow limits of race, religion, class, age, and the like—i.e., within a small pool of eligibles. Another is child marriage. The Hindu prescription was, until very recently, that all girls should be married *before* puberty, and this was the practice as well. In 1891 the average age of females at marriage was 12.5 years. This figure did not rise at all until the decade of the 1930's. It was 14.7 years in 1941.[8] The child has little opportunity to fall in love, and no resources for getting her way if she did. Living with her husband before the marriage was physically consummated, she was more likely to fall in love with him than with anyone else.

A third pattern for controlling love, sometimes linked with the preceding one, specifies rather closely which *status* is to be linked in marriage with which. The traditionally approved marriage among the Bedouin Arabs was between a young man and his father's brother's daughter (*patrilateral parallel cousin marriage*). In most of Arabic Islam this is not the common type of marriage, but in some outlying regions where political power flowed from family linkages, this form made up a majority of marriages. The young man had the right to marry his patrilateral parallel cousin, and would then pay only a nominal bride price. More common is *cross-cousin* marriage, in which usually the boy marries his mother's brother's daughter. When the population of a tribe is small, there may be no one in that "marriage cell." When the kinship group is large, more distant cousins may be treated as "equivalent" and also appropriate, so that some haggling and compromise is still possible. The primary decision however, is *when* the marriage is to occur, since at best only a narrow range of people are permissible or prescribed mates for any given person. These rules also include, of course, various regulations which prohibit marriages with certain kin—i.e., rules of exogamy.

Another method of controlling love relationships is by strict chaperonage, so that young people are simply never permitted to be alone together, or in intimate interaction. Social segregation can best be achieved by physical segregation—for example, the harem system of Islam. In much of Arabic Islam the peasants could not, of course, keep their women in separate quarters, but they could be watched carefully, and were required to wear one of a variety of

---

[8] Shri Nayaran Agarwala, *The Mean Age at Marriage in India as Ascertained from Census Data.* Ph.D. thesis, Princeton University, 1957, Vol. I, Part 2. The data are calculated from *Census of India*, 1891, pp. 155–170; 1941, Papers 1–10.

costumes that hid their faces and bodies from scrutiny. Bedouin Arab girls, on the other hand, ordinarily were permitted some interaction with marriageable men—but they were always under some kind of observation anyway. In China potential spouses were usually selected from families in a different section of a city, or in another village. Most of the young men whom a girl met would belong to the same clan (*tsu*) and would be ineligible for marriage. Upper-class girls were, of course, chaperoned.

Love as an element in marriage selection is becoming more prevalent in all the societies in which it was once uncommon. However, a love pattern certainly existed in at least a large minority of societies even before the recent spread of industrialization. That is, elders did take part in the decision, and had almost a completely free hand in the financial arrangements of the marriage, but young people usually associated prior to marriage, and they decided to marry someone with whom they had fallen in love. Falling in love was not socially prescribed as necessary, but in fact most did so, and married their beloved. This pattern was widespread among the peasantry of Europe prior to industrialization. We have mentioned already the Polynesian societies, where at least the non-nobility were free to engage in love. A substantial number of Melanesian and Papuan societies exhibit such a love pattern, which is also found here and there in Africa (Nuer, Kgatla, Bavenda).

In general, as might be inferred from the preceding discussion, families with a higher social rank grant less freedom in courtship than do families of lower rank. That is, the families that have more to fear from the disruptive effects of love also expend more energy in controlling it.

By channeling love or keeping it under some control, family elders are freer to make marriage bargains with one another. Only where they have the authority to give their sons and daughters in marriage is it possible to maintain a bride-price or dowry system. It becomes pointless to make an agreement whose execution cannot be controlled.

As a consequence, when young people obtain the right to choose their mates themselves, these types of marriage exchanges begin to disappear as an institutionalized element in the agreement to marry. Just why one society has a bride price and another a groom price is not yet known, but some common factors in these two patterns can be found.

Let us first see what each of the relevant terms means. A *dowry* is a sum of money or property that is brought to the marriage by the girl. It is given by her family, but to *whom* it is given varies from one culture to another. In Western countries it was generally given to the groom, who could use it under certain restrictions or even have (under some circumstances) the full disposal of it. In rural Ireland the dowry was in effect given to the groom's father, who then handed over his land to the groom and his bride. The dowry itself was then used to secure a marriage for the groom's sister. Thus, so long as a family had two children or fewer, and no more than one daughter, it could handle the financial problems of marriage. A large dowry was sometimes used to marry a daughter into a higher ranking family—i.e., exchanging money for social rank. Generally, a girl could be considered only if her social skills were adequate for a higher position, and the amount demanded would of course be greater, the higher the rise in rank her family sought. In eighteenth-century France the amounts needed for a given type of alliance were much discussed. In the late nineteenth and early twentieth centuries, many U.S. heiresses married into English or European nobility by furnishing large settlements to their husbands. In contemporary European middle-class society, a dowry is not necessary, but it may smooth the path toward marriage. A *dower* system does not substitute for a dowry system, but is complementary to it, for it is a sum given to the bride by the groom's family, a kind of social security when her husband died. Under the feudal system of Europe and England, she had no rights to her husband's property after his death, though of course it could be expected that if she had a son he would take care of her. Nor did she have any rights to property from her own family. Some women were heiresses, but they were special cases.

Before considering such marriage exchanges in other cultures, several general principles involved in them should be stated. First, which direction the greater value flows expresses the relative evaluation that the society places on the new spouses. In patrilineal African societies, for example, the *lobola*, or bride price, is paid for the children to be born of the mother, and for other wifely duties. Consequently, in matrilineal societies in which the children belong to the mother's line, only a nominal or traditional amount is given. If payment is in the form of groom service, that amount would be small. Brahmins in India had to pay a groom price or dowry in response to a set of forces we shall discuss below.

Second, no matter which direction the greater amount of wealth flows, all such exchanges must even out over time among families or lineages. One family may have more daughters in one generation, but more sons in another. Most marriages occur within the same economic stratum, so that the stratum as a whole gains neither nor loses.

Third, the family receiving more wealth always reciprocates with other gifts, and among the well-to-do it is usually a point of honor to make the counter-gifts about equal in value. Such exchanges are publicly known, and they express both the social rank of the families and their pleasure in the event.

Fourth, whether a dowry or a bride-price system exists, some room for haggling is found within the marriage arrangements. The beautiful, charming girl from a noble family will have to furnish less dowry, while a young man from a noble family may be able to command a large dowry. Or a family may have many daughters, and thus not be able to command so desirable a set of husbands, because their wealth is not sufficient even if they bankrupt themselves. It is to the interest of the elders of the family to drive as good a bargain as possible, but they cannot change the evaluation of the traits of the young spouses they have to offer.

Next, it is clear that as love comes to play a larger role in courtship, so that elders no longer have the power to *execute* the arrangements they make, the dowry and bride price become less important in the courtship system. In addition, of course, young people in love are less disposed to haggle about such matters, and are not motivated to risk delaying the match by driving the best possible bargain for their family elders.

Among Indian Brahmins, the groom price, or dowry, is taken for granted as a necessity, the amount being higher if the man has been well-educated or has a profession. In Hindu society the pattern was enforced by the traditional prescription that a girl must be married before puberty. Consequently, the girl's family was under some time pressure, while the boy's family could wait. In addition, some small amount of hypergamy was permitted, and the girl's family would have to pay for such an upward step. In the Bengal region in the nineteenth century, a Kulin Brahmin man might marry scores of girls from a slightly lower ranking Brahmin caste, receiving gifts with each visit to each wife in addition to the original dowry.

A bride-price system was the pattern followed in China, Japan, Arabic Islam, and most of sub-Sahara Africa. As already noted, the bride price, or *lobola*, expressed the evaluation placed on the wife's future fertility in Africa.

Some analysts have suggested that a bride price added security to the marriage, since the girl's family would have to return it if she would not stay with the man, but if he treated her badly they could refuse. Thus her family would put pressure on her to conform, and his family would keep *his* behavior within permissible limits. Indeed, it is very likely that African systems that stressed *lobola* did have a low divorce rate. However, the causal relationship runs the other way: Families in a system with a low divorce rate (mostly patrilineal) would risk *little* in giving more cattle in their exchanges, since there was little likelihood that the cattle would have to be returned, with the attending annoyance and litigation that were common in such cases. In turn, their women would bring in wealth in exchange when they married. On the other hand, systems with high divorce rates would stipulate only a small bride price since elders would not wish to risk such an investment. This proposition obviously applies to the dowry system in the Western nations as well.

Islamic law had one striking trait that set the Arab custom apart from most other bride price systems. In poor families the bride's father was likely to take most of the bride price, while in middle- or upper-class families she was likely to obtain most of it, and in addition the groom's family made gifts to her. Whatever the amount of wealth from these two sources, it remained legally hers within the marriage, and her husband could not dispose of it in any way without her permission. If under the marriage agreement he did not pay all of the bride price at marriage, he was bound to pay the remainder if they divorced. This meant that when she returned to her parental home at the time of divorce she also brought back her wealth with her. Once back, she remained a potential source of further wealth which would come in the form of another bride price from a different husband.

forms
of the household
five

Almost all the world's population lives in family units, but the structures or forms vary not only from one society to another but also from one class to another within the same society. These variations result from many accidental, idiosyncratic, and normative factors. In the U.S., about 11 per cent of all households are "one-person" units, while about 1 per cent contain ten or more persons. Both of these extremes are viewed as permissible in the society, but neither represents the ideal of the society—i.e., a married couple alone, or a married couple with children. Interestingly enough, just half of all families in 1960 were made up of a married couple living in their own household with children under 18 years of age, and without any other relatives or lodgers in the household.[1]

Implications of Household Forms

The various forms of the household have a number of implications for family interaction. They help to determine, for example, the chances of more or less intimate social relations among members of the kinship group. Thereby, these structural patterns shape in part the processes of strain

[1] U.S. Census of Population, *Families, 1960* (Washington, D.C.: U.S. Bureau of the Census, 1963), p. 21.

and adjustment among relatives. Various role relations may have to be spelled out in detail, if the household includes certain relatives. For example, if the household usually includes a man and his mother-in-law, there may be rules requiring much reserve or *non*interaction between the two.

Socialization patterns are also affected by who is included in the household. A mother-in-law may continue to supervise the socialization of a young daughter-in-law, or a young boy may go to his mother's brother's house to grow up. A young child in a polygynous household sees a wider range of adult models intimately than he could observe in a nuclear family. Those who share the same household are likely to share the same budget, and thus economic exchanges are partly determined by the forms of the household.

What are the main family forms to be considered? The *nuclear* family is a unit composed of husband, wife, and their children. *Polygyny* and *polyandry* are the two types of polygamy. In the first, one man has two or more wives, so that the household is made up of two or more nuclear families, in which the same man is the husband. A common form is *sororal* polygyny, in which a man marries two or more sisters. In polyandry, one woman is wife to two or more men, but of course there is only one set of children. A widespread form, called *fraternal* polyandry, is the marriage of one woman to a set of brothers.

The household may be enlarged *generationally* as well as laterally by the addition of other nuclear units. The term *extended* family is loosely applied to a system in which the ideal of the society is that several generations should live under one roof. Usually, it refers to a system such as the Chinese in which a man and his wife live with the families of their married sons, with their un-married sons and daughters, and of course with any grandchildren or great-grandchildren in the paternal line. A large or extended family may also be made up of the family units a man forms with his several wives, together with the families his sons found, as in many African and Arab societies. All may live together in a compound, great house, or in tents close together.

This term "extended," is less often applied to the *stem* family, common in feudal and post-feudal Europe, among some immigrant farmer groups here and there in the U.S., and in Tokugawa Japan. Under this system only one child, usually the eldest son, inherited the family property; and he had some responsi-bility for his sisters until they married, and for his brothers until they were grown. Thus the property, family title, and responsibility were in the hands of one person.

The *joint* family of India is sometimes called "extended," but it is best to use the more specific term. It is made up of *co-parceners*—that is, persons who have a right to the products of the family property. These are the brothers in any generation, together with their sons in the next generation, plus sons of the third generation. That is, it includes all the brothers in each generation in a direct line, from a given set of brothers, as long as the unit is still intact. The emphasis was placed on the brothers, since under Hindu tradition a male child had from its birth a right in the family property. This type of property, called *coparcenary*, has become less common in modern India. Although the family members who were supposed to be in the household were not significantly dif-ferent from those expected to be in the Chinese household, the status of the property was different, since coparcenary property could not ordinarily be divided, whereas Chinese property was usually divided among the sons on their father's death. In addition, even if Hindu brothers live separately they consider themselves a joint family if they continue to respect their common obligations, which include a joint budget, authority in the hands of the oldest male, and joint maintenance of the property. The oldest male, who is the head of the family, cannot dispose of the property. In 1956 the legal status of this unit was changed to include sisters and widow as entitled to a share in the property.

Of course, rules of *residence* may affect the composition of the household. In the U.S. *neolocality* is the rule, for it is considered proper that a young married couple set up a new residence, apart from either parental home. In matrilineal societies (i.e., in which descent is traced through the mother's line), the couple is expected to reside near the wife's family, or sometimes within their household. This rule is generally called *matrilocality*, although perhaps a more precise term is *uxorilocality*, suggesting residence near the wife's home. The residence rule that accompanies patrilineality is *patrilocality*, and again the new family unit may become part of the groom's father's household.

The rules of residence determine in part who associates with whom after marriage. If a man moves to take up residence near his wife and her lineage, the likelihood increases that he will have frequent social interaction with her kin. Residence rules also affect another set of relations. In any society whose economy depends partly on hunting, trapping, lumbering, quarrying, or fishing, the man who moves far would thereby render less useful some of his localized, geographical knowledge. In most societies, residence is patrilocal, but where it is matrilocal the man rarely moves to a new community—i.e., some distance away. Instead he moves to a different part of the village, near his wife's relatives.[2] In a few instances the group is migratory anyway, within a territory which he knows well. Of course, the woman's skills are scarcely affected by moving close to her husband's paternal relatives. In societies in which she does move, however, there is more likelihood of a bride price being paid, whereas in a matrilocal or uxorilocal system it is unlikely that a substantial bride price would be demanded. Her skills really would not be lost to her family, and thus no compensation would be required.

Incidence of Household Forms

Before analyzing some of the further traits of these various forms of the family, let us first ask how common they are. If we define a society as polygynous when the *ideal* is for a man to acquire two or more wives, then a majority are polygynous: 193 out of 234 societies in Murdock's sample.[3] On the other hand, only one of the numerically great civilizations of the world is polygynous—Islam. China, Japan, India, and the West are not. Murdock has also calculated the number of societies in which as many as 20 per cent of the unions are polygynous, and concludes that about 70 per cent of the polygynous societies are above the 20 per cent line. Unfortunately, these figures must be estimates, since many ethnographic reports do not contain an actual count of such household units.

Polygyny as an ideal has perhaps been more widespread in Africa than in any other region—in 88 per cent of the 154 sub-Sahara tribes for which data are available.[4] In a recent careful evaluation of Africa, it was estimated that 1 out of 3 males was or is polygynous, and that the mean number of wives per married man was 1.5.[5]

Only under very special circumstances it is possible for even a majority

---

2 George P. Murdock, *Social Structure* (New York: Macmillan, 1949), pp. 213–214.
3 *Ibid.*, p. 28.
4 George P. Murdock, *Africa* (New York: McGraw-Hill, 1959), p. 25.
5 Vernon R. Dorjahn, "The Factor of Polygamy in African Demography," in William R. Bascom and Melville J. Herskovits (eds.), *Continuity and Change in African Cultures* (Chicago: University of Chicago Press, 1959), pp. 102–105.

of men to have more than one wife at a time. At birth, males outnumber females slightly, about 103:100 (this is called the *sex ratio*), and in subsequent years the mortality rate is higher among males. However, females outnumber males substantially only in the later years of life, long after the normal age at marriage. Polygyny is impossible unless a society loses a large segment of its males through war, or captures many women.

Some part of the discrepancy between ideal and reality is made up by marrying girls early in life, and men late in life. Thus, if females marry at age 14, and males at age 25, a surplus of 9 marital years per female is created, to be distributed among the men who are able to acquire another wife.

In many polygynous societies additional wives need not be a financial burden. In most African tribes, for example, women work at agriculture or trading, and may actually earn more than they and their children cost. As in other economic enterprises, however, some initial capital is necessary. A man whose kin cannot secure a sufficient bride price, or whose personal resources are insufficient, cannot obtain secondary wives even though they would not be an economic burden. Perhaps more important, in few societies do all men have the *right* to additional wives, even when they are able and willing to pay for them. A man may be criticized for "stepping out of place" if he acquires another wife when his social rank is thought to be low. An older man of station, or a politically powerful one, may, however, enlarge his entourage of wives as a validation of his status, or to cement an alliance with another family or political figure. In a hunting economy, such as the Eskimo, a second wife betokens the prowess of the great hunter who needs more than one wife in order to take care of all the skins and meat he brings home.

As already mentioned, in most major civilizations few men have had to cope with the problem, or enjoyed the possible delights, of polygyny. But though large households formed by polygyny have not been the norm in these great civilizations, they might have been created through residence rules that urged young men not to leave the parental home when they marry. So much is this the ideal that in the recent past the usual descriptions of the Chinese, Arab, or Indian family systems show the extended family as the usual mode of living. A consideration of the evidence suggests that the reality is more complex, and that this form of household was instead more common among well-to-do families. Let us look at the evidence, and then analyze some of the consequences of the extended household for the life of its members. In China, a man could bring a concubine into his household. Some scholars consider these women to have been at least "secondary wives," since various laws and legal rulings defined their social status, as well as that of their children as members of the family. The process of taking a concubine was close to a genuine purchase, and only the rich could afford one. Japan was also legally monogamous, but a successful man might purchase a concubine. Polygyny was possible in India, but Hindu law did not support the practice, and few men had more than one wife at a time. Under Islamic law a man might have as many as four wives, and many men married more than once. But most had only one wife at a time.

In modern China, and very likely in past periods as well, only the well-to-do were able to maintain an extended family network in one household: The greater the size of the farm, the greater the size of a household. In one survey in 1942, the average household size ranged from 4.1 persons in Jehol Province to a high of 6.9 in the frontier province of Kirin in Manchuria. This range makes it unlikely that the extended household combining several nuclear families was the typical family form. In a broad survey conducted during the 1920's

(Ting Hsien) the average was 5.8 persons. This probably is not a modern trend. The average family may have included only about five to six persons throughout much of the past 2,000 years.[6]

Why has the ideal not been followed? Certainly the patriarch, surrounded by his married sons and his grandsons, was accorded much esteem in China. The answer points to several factors that affect household composition in most societies. Sons could demand a division of the property after their father's death, and some wives pressed them to do so. Mortality took its toll among the older and the younger generations, reducing the number in the household. Only a few men with considerable land or a good business could offer adequate economic opportunities to all their sons or grandsons, so that all might remain in the great household after marriage.

Thus, against the gradual accretion of new members is set a constant process of fission or dissolution.

In the Arab family system, both polygyny and the retention of the married sons in the family might have built up very large households, and it is likely that until recently most Arabs lived in such a household at *some* time in their lives, if only briefly. At any given time, on the other hand, most did not. Among the desert Bedouin, a young man was usually given a tent of his own when he married. In the 1920's in Syria, even in the large cities, there were a few large households of 40 or more members, though they were not common.

Data from one Egyptian province, Sharquia, show, however, that even in the 1880's the average family size was 5.5 members. In 1917 only one-third of Egyptian families had as many as 6 to 10 members, and 60 per cent had 1 to 5 members, hardly consonant with the traditional picture of the great extended household. In 1947 the average size of the Egyptian family was 4.8 members. In 1950, in a survey among several small population groups in Morocco, the average size of the household was 4.0 members. For Algeria as a whole, the average was 5.1 members in 1954. Other census and survey data yield similar results, undermining the assumption that most Arab households were comprised of several generations of families in the male line.

The case of India deserves detailed attention, because in the 1950's scholars debated among themselves as to how prevalent the joint family was in India, and thus how much industrialization or urbanization had affected the family system.

In the 1951 census, less than 6 per cent of Indian families had 10 members or more, whereas 34 per cent had 3 members or less, and 43 per cent had 4 to 6 members. Since 77 per cent of the families had 6 members or less, a genuine joint family would seem to have been uncommon, since it would presumably be made up of an adult couple, their unmarried sons and daughters, and their married sons together with these sons' wives and children. So small a figure might suggest a change from the past, if the large household was once common. In harmony with this notion, in 1951 a larger percentage of small households were to be found in Indian *cities* than in rural regions, and a higher percentage of large households (7 to 9 members) in rural areas.

Interpreted plausibly, these data show that the joint family has declined. Unfortunately, this interpretation is weakened by the fact that the census of 1901 *also* reported a small average household size—5 persons. Averages in various Indian states ranged from 4.4 in Ajmar to 6.2 in the Punjab. Moreover, even at

6 Morton H. Fried, "The Family in China: The People's Republic," in Ruth N. Anshen (ed.), *The Family*, rev. ed. (New York: Harper, 1959), p. 148. See also Maurice Freedman, *Lineage Organization in Southeastern China* (London: Athlone Press, 1958), p. 3, for additional studies on the size of the Chinese household.

forms of the household

that time, before any substantial effect of urbanization or industrialization could have occurred, the colonial rulers were commenting that the joint family was not so common as had been supposed.

The joint family cannot be dismissed as a myth, however, First, to the extent that it is an *ideal*, men who achieve rank and wealth will establish such a household. The resulting association between class position and the large household will maintain the high evaluation placed on this family form. Second, it is possible that even when members of an extended kinship network do not live in the same household, they may share a common budget and follow the same family leader. Third, possibly *most* members of a population may live in such a joint household at some time in their lives, as their families pass through the *phase* of being joint.

It seems likely that the Indian family fits both the first and third possibilities, and to some extent the second as well.

The Indian Joint Family

An examination of the Indian joint family throws light on these possibilities and on the problems to be found in all extended families. As mentioned earlier, the joint family is based on the relations among adult males, rather than on the conjugal bonds between *spouses*. Arranged marriages lower the likelihood that an intense marriage bond might break up the unit into nuclear households. Segregation of the sexes before and after marriage further lessens the chance of such a breakup. An emphasis on respect between generations, rather than a full expression of love, is illustrated by the norms governing overt expressions of tenderness by the father toward his son. The father is not supposed to express tenderness in the presence of other adult males; since houses are small, this means that most of the time others *are* present. Husband and wife too should not show much affection toward each other, unless they are alone. In households following traditional norms, men eat first. There is also a norm that requires the adult male to take care of all his dependents, not only his own children. Thus, many rules block the normal tendency of the nuclear family to break away and to form a separate household.

There are also many pressures toward fission. Wives do not have the same allegiance toward the large unit that their husbands feel, and may come to believe that their husbands contribute more than they receive, that their children are deprived of a fair share, and that adjustment to so many others is too difficult. The joint family cares for the lazy as well as the helpless, but the woman with diligent sons may not be willing to take care of the less deserving.

Moreover, serious problems of integration and authority are created by the need to keep many people organized within the same household. Before the contemporary period, the father's authority was not likely to be challenged, nor that of the oldest brother if he was considerably older than the rest. However, challenges are more likely to appear as soon as efficiency or technical knowledge becomes the basis of decisions. An educated younger brother, for example, may be able to give better advice on jobs and schools than the oldest male in the household.

Sometimes social mobility also decreases joint family solidarity. A man may have risen to a high occupation through the support given to him by his uncles, but becomes reluctant to share all his income with the larger family. When all are at the same level, sharing may mean exchanging equally; when only *one* is rich, "sharing" means paying out constantly.

Nevertheless, the ideal of remaining together is strong, and fission is unlikely unless the father dies or all the brothers have become adult. Men may blame their wives, rather than admit that for selfish reasons they want to set up separate households.

Considering these conflicting forces, it is not surprising, then, that surveys over the past decade show that a majority of Indian families live in nuclear households; but it is not certain whether or not these families *operate* jointly—i.e., pool their income or accept the authority of the oldest male, though living in physically separate households. At present the data suggest that most families do not operate jointly, but are linked by a keener sense of mutual obligations and a more intense loyalty to distant relatives than are families in the West.

On the other hand, very likely a high percentage of Indian families do go through a joint *phase*. To consider this possibility, let us follow a hypothetical Indian couple throughout their married life. First, they establish a nuclear unit within a larger household, the family of the groom's father. Soon after marriage, the birth of a first child, or the death of the groom's father, the young man may separate his own family from the larger household. His departure may be late or early, depending on job opportunities, his education, or the scarcity of resources within the household. If the young man leaves late in his *own* marriage, then very likely his *father's* household has by then become joint—i.e., it contains some married brothers, their wives and offspring, and possibly some members of the older generation (in modern India, these may also include relations who are *not* part of the direct male line). After the young man leaves, he may be able to hold his own sons together until they marry and have children, thus for a time forming a joint household.

The Indian tradition favors the creation of a joint family, and public-opinion polls in most areas show that most people are still in favor of such a family form, although a substantial minority are in favor of living separately. In general, urban residents are less strongly in favor of the joint family than are rural residents, and the educated less than the uneducated.

Perhaps more important is the fact that such polls do *not* distinguish the *type* of joint family preferred (father-sons or brothers without the father). Very likely, a majority of Indians would not be in favor of brothers living together after the father's death, and almost certainly a majority of married women would not be, since they normally bear the burden of adjustment in such a unit.

Strengths of the Extended Family

Thus the large extended household grows and declines over the years as it is affected by fertility, marriage and divorce, mortality, residence rules, and the alternative opportunities open to its members. Its importance is to be found in the advantages it offers under certain types of circumstances. Since the extended family may be viewed as a kind of social invention, let us see what its strengths and weaknesses are.

First, the extended family is most likely to be found in non-urban, non-industrialized settings, because it can furnish social services that are usually lacking in societies without many specialized agencies and organizations. In other words, people who live in extended families can turn to many other people for help. The aged, the ill, the crippled, and infirm are less a burden on the large extended family than on a nuclear or conjugal family, since their cost to each active member is less. As an extreme contrast, consider the former custom among the Eskimos, who abandoned the non-productive older members from their conjugal family systems when food was short. The pattern in African societies by which a man inherits the wives of another man was in part a social-security measure to insure elderly support for widows as long as they lived. Of course, in all societies without systems of public welfare the non-productive are the responsibility of the family, but the extended household can more easily discharge this burden than can a smaller type of family unit.

The extended household, in spite of its turnover, is more durable than the conjugal household. Individuals come and go, but the unit maintains its identity and property and its collective responsibility. The death or absence of the mother or father in the conjugal or nuclear family seriously impairs or even destroys its effectiveness.

The extended family is also better able to amass the capital for an important economic enterprise, whether it is obtaining enough cattle for a marriage, buying land or a governmental office, or paying for the education of a young man of promise. As long as those who receive the benefit of the investment also continue to feel obliged to share that benefit with their kinsmen, the group as a whole can function as a kind of savings bank. Of course, the conjugal family has to apportion its rewards among fewer people, but correspondingly there are fewer people from whom to obtain support when investment capital is needed. One important consequence of this fact is that in the first stages of industrialization in a new country, upper-strata families are likely to be still better off economically than their fellow citizens. Having an extended kinship network to call on, they are better able to invest in new types of enterprise.

In societies where all adult men are at least potentially warriors, the large extended family will have more political influence than the small conjugal family. The threat of violence may not confer legitimacy, but it often bestows some power. A family head who can call on a goodly number of followers from his own family is likely to be accorded more attention than the head of a small family unit. One consequence, especially among the upper strata of most societies, is that negotiations leading to marriage are frequently concerned with the possible political fruitfulness of new alliances. Of course, with the establishment of formal agencies of the law, and a more effective police system, this protective support of the extended family becomes less important, and this family form becomes less common.

The Western Conjugal Family

It is appropriate at this point to consider in more detail the conjugal, or nuclear, family of the modern urban Western countries. Either term may be used interchangeably when referring to the family unit itself, but the term "conjugal" is preferable when referring to the family system as a whole. No nuclear family *system* exists, if by that we mean a system in which most families maintain few or no relations with their more extended kin. All contemporary studies in the most industrialized countries—Great Britain and the U.S.—show that in fact each family unit maintains contact with a wide range of relatives, and that the largest single category of "recreation" is "visiting with relatives." In addition, it is easy to see that many of these relatives *outside* the conjugal unit cannot be cut off without annoying or hurting someone *inside* the family, simply because each person in the family is or will be a member of two families simultaneously. A son cannot rebuff his father's father or mother, father's brother, or father's sister, without angering his father. Nor can he be hostile toward his nephews or nieces without also rebuffing his sister or brother.

Thus, at present it seems useful to keep in mind that a conjugal family system is one in which more social emphasis is placed on the conjugal bond, or on the structural form of the nuclear family, than in other family systems, but the small family unit is not entirely independent.

The fact that the conjugal family is less dependent than other family units on the wider kinship network has a wide range of implications, which we shall briefly review here. Since most affinal (in-laws) and consanguineal (blood) kin are *relatively* excluded from the conjugal family's day-to-day decisions, neither those kin nor the small family unit can count on much societal support for a regular flow of services or help from each other. That is, the larger society does not require much exchange of this kind. Consequently, both extended kin and the nuclear family unit have a weaker basis for social controls over one another, for they cannot force compliance by reward or punishment.

Since these mandatory exchanges are fewer, and reciprocal controls are weaker, there are fewer pressures on the new couple to settle near their relatives after marriage. Neolocality, in turn, supports the relative independence of the small family unit.

Next, neither the bride's nor the groom's family is likely to gain much from the marriage (because custom does not demand many economic or social exchanges), so choice of mate is relatively free. Adjustment between husband and wife takes precedence over that among relatives, or between couple and relatives. Consequently, the relatively excluded kin do not attempt to assert much control over who marries whom.

The conjugal system is multilineal or bilineal, rather than unilineal, at least in the sense that *neither* the female nor the male line is given much priority. Emphasis on the *marital* bond between husband and wife reduces the possibility of a lineage system, or of any other large corporate kin grouping based on a line of descent. Neolocality also makes the maintenance of a social emphasis on one kin line rather difficult, since many couples may live too far away from the rest of the lineage to be able to take part in joint activities or rituals.

Equally important is the intensity of emotionality within the conjugal family unit. The conjugal family is founded on mutual attraction and love. It is made up of a small number of people in close contact with one another. The emotional ties among members of the large extended household are likely to be diffuse and less intense. This degree of emotionality in the conjugal unit is accentuated by the fact that custom forbids the individual to go anywhere else in the society for solace. This creates both the intimacy and the fragility of the conjugal family. If the husband or wife do not in fact obtain love and comfort within the family unit, then they have little motivation to continue to support it. Thus the divorce rate in the conjugal family system is likely to be high.

Finally, since this type of system contains no large kinship groupings that offer various social-welfare services, it has no simple way of taking care of the dependent, the helpless, or the aged. Orphanages or similar organizations may be necessary, since many children lose their parents, and no corporate kinship unit is responsible for supporting them. Homes for the aged, as well as complex social-security measures, must substitute for the assumption of this burden by the kinship network in other systems. Correlatively, those who are widowed, widowered, or divorced are likely to remarry, since their kin have no collective responsibility for taking care of them and their children.

On the other hand, such a system may fit the needs of an industrial system better than many other family forms. This problem will be analyzed in more detail in a later chapter.

Weaknesses of the Extended Family

If the extended family household possesses these advantages, why is it not the prevalent form in all or most societies? A partial answer might be that where there are lineages—i.e., *corporate* kinship groups

forms of the household

based on a principle of descent, such as patriliny—these larger groups are still more effective than an extended family in precisely these areas. A secondary partial answer would be that the extended family is less prevalent in societies that develop the more impersonal organizations for lending money, keeping the peace, helping the poor, or carrying out collective enterprises of some magnitude.

Neither of these partial answers, however, deals with the question of why so few families are large extended units, even in the societies that evaluate this family form highly. The answer lies in the inner dynamics of such a group, and its relation to the larger social structure. Some of these factors have already been mentioned in passing, but should be repeated here.

First, the integration of so many people into a single unit requires managerial skills and leadership, even when most of the members' duties are traditionally assigned. Usually, it requires both a strong older woman to organize the internal flow of services and food, and a strong man to assume over-all direction of the unit and of relations with other parts of the society. Often the male head is not the ablest man in the family, and the latter is prevented from assuming the post because of traditional rules. Strong men or women may refuse to cooperate with the formal head of the family.

Second, although such a grouping can take care of the infirm or incompetent, it has no way of ridding itself of this burden, and sometimes the cost weighs heavily on total income. A wealthy family may spoil its sons. They, in turn, may drain its income, and eventually dissipate the family fortune.

Perhaps most important, the large household can stay together only as long as its land or other wealth can support it and it can offer adequate opportunities to the younger generation. If it grows, without a commensurate increase in its control over political posts, jobs, land, or military opportunities, members of the family must go elsewhere to found families of their own. In one study of Arab families in Israel, it was found that no son who was sole heir to the land ever had broken away from the parental hearth to form a family of his own. Since most families cannot maintain themselves at a high level of power and wealth from one generation to another, the extended unit is likely to break up over time. If the large household can hold together, it obtains some advantages, but it cannot control all the factors in the larger society that permit it to hold together. Nor can a conjugal family unit without great luck or talent manage to amass the wealth or political power that will permit it to grow into a large extended family unit. Consequently, we should not expect that in *any* society a majority of families will be of the extended type, even when most members of the society aspire to live in or to found such a family.

Inner Dynamics of the Extended Household

Let us now consider further the inner dynamics of the extended household. Several sociological generalizations apply to the patterns of interaction among its members. The most obvious fact is that the *number* and *kinds* of social relations increase geometrically with an increase in the number of people in the unit. Each person not only must take into account a larger number of *people* but also a larger number of social *relations*. That is, if the family grows by the addition of a new wife, the others will not only enter into social relations with her but must also take into account all the relations she establishes with others.

This is a formal trait of the extended family unit, but with it will be found a number of social regularities. One is the increased likelihood of *structural differentiation* within the family. That is, a greater number of kinship labels or terms will be found, and a clearer recognition of formal authority. Rules of avoidance or reserve are more common. The large household becomes like a small community, and there may be much delegation of authority, division of labor, and the like.

Next, an individual cannot spend as much of his time with any *one* person as he might in a small conjugal family. His day is divided among far more people. Social analysts generally agree that one consequence of this dispersion of social energy and interaction is a lessened *intensity* of emotional ties between any two individuals. It is therefore likely, in harmony with the preceding paragraph, that there will be more rules that specify the frequency and type of role interaction that each individual owes to others. These obligations cannot be left to individual preference alone, or to accidental encounter. In polygynous households, for example, rules specify how a man shall spend his nights with his wives, usually visiting each in rotation and including the old and less comely so as to avoid humiliating them. And, as we said earlier, there may also be rules of avoidance. For example, a young wife may be required to avoid being in a room alone with her father-in-law, or to avoid speaking to him; or a young husband may be prohibited from speaking to or using the name of his mother-in-law. Rules of avoidance do reduce possible friction in a limited living space. They are also sometimes interpreted as a mechanism for lowering the possibility of sexual relations between certain categories of people.

The members of an extended household are, of course, highly *visible* to one another—i.e., they see one another more frequently than they would if the constituent nuclear families each had their own separate household. More people have the right and obligation to *watch* one another, to be concerned about one another's behavior. There is a lack of privacy, which means that any individual who deviates is more likely to be exposed. Everything is everybody's business, and no one can go unscolded or unminded. As a further consequence, we should expect greater *consensus* among the members of the extended household, concerning what is right and proper, than among the same families if they lived separately. This process of continued re-affirmation of common values partly counterbalances the threatened conflict that is generated by the sheer number of different people, in many different social statuses, who thus have somewhat different interests to pursue.

This process of social control has been of special importance in the socialization of the bride in such cultures as China, India, and the Arab countries.

The process by which consensus is attained in the large extended family is rendered somewhat complicated in some societies by a phenomenon that has been accorded scant attention in research and writing on the family—the practice of child-switching. It was common in medieval England, and among Puritans until late in the colonial period in the U.S., for parents to send their young children to live with kinfolk. The Puritans thought of this as a way by which the natural tendency of parents to indulge and spoil their children could be neutralized. The children would receive good training in a good family, among kin who would not exploit them.

This pattern cannot, however, be ascribed to the supposed harshness of Puritan parents, since clearly it grew from an older English tradition. Moreover, it is relatively common in Africa, where often (as among the Kongo) the son was sent to live with the mother's brother, at about the age of 6 to 10 years. Among the Haida of the Pacific Northwest, too, the boy might grow up to marry his mother's brother's daughter, after having spent his late childhood in that family. Such a system helps to integrate the child into the larger community, of course, but raises interesting problems concerning the transfer of affection and identification from one set of adults to another.

We have mentioned the possibility of conflict that arises from the simple fact of a large number of people occupying the same living space, but one specific type of conflict should be considered here. In polygynous systems with a preference for sororal polygyny, all the sisters may live together; but it is common for wives who are not sisters to be segregated from one another in separate rooms or even separate huts. Whatever the physical arrangements, some problems of authority can arise. The newer and younger wife may receive more favors and attention from the husband. The elder wife is likely to have come from a higher-ranking family than the others, and to be given more authority. The husband must delegate some responsibility to one wife, and this may create resentment.

Equally important is the problem of inheritance. Each mother will attempt to obtain favors for her children, and to persuade the husband to make her son (usually the oldest) the main heir. Rules of inheritance are often not specific enough to eliminate all threats of conflict among mothers. The history of African kingdoms is studded with fraternal violence—half-brothers fighting with half-brothers for a chieftaincy, one consequence of this battle for place and power.

Finally, in all societies that place a high evaluation on some form of the extended family, the elders are paid great deference and prestige. Not all such societies have been non-literate. In none, however, have living patterns been regulated primarily by technical or scientific learning, so the accumulation of folk wisdom by the elders has not been thought of as an ornament alone, but as a necessity—the ways of a tiger, when to plant, how to approach a high official or to conduct delicate marriage negotiations. The young could not easily outstrip the old in such knowledge. The elders' advantage also has stemmed from their responsibility for rituals. They have also been considered closest to the gods because of the imminence of their death, and thus deserving of respect and authority. As we mentioned earlier, the unit cost of maintaining the old is low in such systems, and the absolute cost is low because so few live to be very old.

Finally, it has been to the interest of people at intermediate ages or statuses to support the old, to maintain the system, for they know that in time they too will grow old. If these intermediate people challenge the authority of the old too soon, or supplant them without finesse and respect, then they undermine the structure which they could otherwise enjoy in their own old age. Indeed, the consequences of according no clear status to the old may be seen in our own society, where the problems of the aged are viewed as increasingly difficult to solve.

organized
descent groupings
six

In all past societies, the links of kinship have been recognized beyond the confines of the nuclear or composite family unit. If recognition extended so far as to include everyone who is related by blood, though however distant a tie, clearly everyone would be considered a relative of everyone else. The network of kinship is definitely extensible. Thus if one wished to create various organizations to take care of a wide range of activities beyond the capacities of the individual family, such as maintaining temples, conducting religious rituals, administering a market, or furnishing labor for road-building, people could be chosen to participate in such organizations on the basis of their position in a kinship network. Indeed, this type of social invention has been widespread, and has been identified by various labels, such as lineages, clans, kindreds, and so on.

Different principles could be used to divide the population by kinship position. Only the maternal line might be used, or only the paternal, or some combination of the two. Perhaps sisters might be allocated to the maternal line, and brothers to the paternal. Notice, however, that what distinguishes our own type of kinship system from most others is not which descent *principle* is used, but the fact that certain kin are *organized*, and have collective duties and rights. Patrilineal descent is given more recognition than matrilineal descent in Western society—for example, perhaps most readers of this volume will know their father's father's father's name, but few will know their mother's mother's mother's name. However, those who are related through the male line do not own property together, nor are they even socially recognized as members of any grouping.

Patrilineage: An Example

Since it is the rare Western reader who has had any experience of living even briefly in such a kinship unit, perhaps an exercise of the imagination is necessary to understand it. Let us suppose we had patrilineages in this country.

First, almost everyone would be a member of some lineage. Second, how many lineages there would be would depend on how far back one's ancestry would be traced—with a literate tradition and concern for records, perhaps eventually ten generations or so. The greater the generational depth of a lineage, the fewer the number of lineages needed to include the entire population. Perhaps a few hundred might contain the population of the U.S. These might, in turn, be linked in still larger groupings of lineages, called clans. Extensive lineages might be segmented into sub-lineages.

Third, who would be included in your lineage? Since it would be patrilineal, you would include all your male ancestors in the direct line. In only a few patrilineage systems is the wife viewed as having joined the lineage by marriage. In any event, your father's brothers would be included, and his sons and daughters. Also included would be your father's father, his brothers, and their male descendents plus all their male siblings and these siblings' descendents—i.e., the *collaterals*. Only the descendents of the males would be included. The descendents of females would be included in the lineages of the men these women married. In effect, the lineage is composed of all the descendents of a founding father and his wife or wives.

Would your family and kinship behavior be different from what it is today, when the ordinary American family head interacts with scores of in-laws and blood kin over a period of months? With reference to most of your actions with*in* the nuclear family, little change would be evident, although your father would have somewhat more authority than at present. With reference to matters *out*side the nuclear family, however, some changes would occur. Most important, your relatives through your mother's family would play a smaller part in your life. You would expect less help from them, and you would be less anxious about incurring their possible displeasure. Of course, as in all societies, if they lived very close to you, they would nevertheless be rather important to you.

Next, if you were old enough to marry, the patrilineage would have a hand in the marriage—setting rules concerning whom you might marry (e.g., you could not marry a first cousin if she were a co-member), helping to amass the money for the marriage celebration and setting up the household—perhaps even picking out your spouse. If you were male, you would claim your children for the lineage in the event of divorce, since they would be members of it from birth. If you were female, you would have to return to your family without your children.

At various religious rituals, your lineage might have certain responsibilities, such as furnishing members to execute the rituals, or helping to pay for them. If you traveled to another city, you would expect to be received with open arms by fellow members of your lineage. If you had a serious quarrel with a fellow member, the elders of the lineage would adjudicate the issue rather than permit

57

you to go to court. If your serious conflict were with an outsider, the lineage would support your side of the quarrel.

In general, in your role relations *outside* your own household, you would be treated as a member of a lineage rather than as an independent individual. Under such a system you would lose some of your present freedom to interact or not with certain kin, but you would gain some security and protection, from the unity of your patrilineal kin. Finally, many important activities of the society would be the responsibility of one lineage or another.

Kinship Groupings and the Family

Since these kinship structures go *beyond* the family, do they properly belong in an analysis of the family? Traditionally, family sociologists pay little attention to them; and anthropologists are likely to think of them less as a part of family interaction than as the main constituent of the larger social structure itself.

At a minimum, however, in assessing the importance of the family, it seems necessary to understand how the elementary social relations of kinship are used as the building stones of more complex social structures which carry out important societal tasks. Next, membership in kinship collectives often defines who may or may not marry whom. For example, most lineages are exogamous—i.e., one may not marry within it. A third justification for examining corporate kinship units here is that the individual family, and especially the husband-wife bond, is less likely to be the prime unit in social interaction where such units are well-developed—though of course membership in the descent group is determined in turn by family patterns.

Also, many duties relating to the family are based *outside* the family. For example, among the matrilineal Trobrianders, the wife's brother furnished yams for her family. Both were joined in the same lineage with her children. She had some claim to the produce from the land he held, and so did her children, who in turn had no claim to their father's landholdings, since they were not his heirs. Later, we shall discuss other features of a matrilineage, but here we are merely noting that family obligations may have their origin outside the family.

Finally, the family is the source of the loyalties and commitments on which the descent grouping must be able to count. Rights and duties are couched in a rhetoric of the family. Notice, as a vestige of this, the former rural pattern in the U.S. of calling distant relatives "cousin" or "uncle," to express kinship solidarity and friendship.

As already suggested in the previous discussion, the lineage is only one form of the organized descent grouping. The main modes of tracing descent are *unilineal* and *omnilineal*.[1] Some systems combine both unilineal principles, so that a person's kinship position is fixed by both his maternal and paternal lines. In a lineage an individual can trace his relationship to any co-member, by their tie to a known *common* ancestor, as well as to the known founding ancestor. Thus, in a patrilineage, an individual and his cousins on his father's side both have a common grandfather, and are the same number of generations removed from the ancestor who founded the patrilineage.

In a *clan* the difference is that two clan members may not be able to trace out their exact kinship relation to one another, especially if they are distant kin, since not all the generations between the founding ancestor and the

[1] In an unpublished mimeographed exposition, Dr. Michael Banton of the University of Edinburgh has presented one of the clearest discussions of the main ideas in current analyses of descent. "Omnilineal" is a term suggested by Max Gluckman.

organized descent groupings

present generation are clearly charted. Usually the clan has a name, such as Wolf, Beaver, or Owl, whereas lineages often do not have a specific label. The founding ancestor of a clan may also be mythical, the offspring of a human being and an animal. Clans often exist without lineages, but the latter are sometimes united into clans, which usually contain a residentially unified, unilineal core of kin.

If descent is traced through both lines in each ascending generation, as in the modern West, we may call it omnilineal, multilineal, or "bilateral." Consanguineal ties in any direction are recognized. This descent grouping is called a *kindred*, which recognizes blood ties in all directions—close to what rural people sometimes call their "kinfolk." This type will be discussed later in this chapter.

The main functions (in the sense of "consequences") of such organized kinship groupings are important for both the larger society and the family, since they are the intermediate links between the two. Some of these functions were mentioned in Chapter 5. The corporate descent group can protect the individual family politically, since it can muster a greater number of men. It can act as a collective banker as well as tax collector, demanding of each family some contribution for a necessary collective enterprise, which might range from a marriage to the clearing of new land for growing crops. Often the chief religious rituals are organized and executed by the descent-group leaders.

All these activities transcend both the interest and the power of the individual family. The family may wish the rituals to be performed, but could not and would not pay for all their cost. If a young man is to be married, his own family is interested; but his kin are only mildly interested, and would contribute only little to the cost. However, a lineage can, as it were, focus both interest and contribution on a necessary task.

A further function can be discerned from the relationships just noted. By virtue of the descent-group links, the family is drawn more firmly into the larger society. If very serious, its quarrels must be submitted to the adjudication of clan or lineage elders. It cannot deviate too widely from community norms, because it must continue to fulfill its collective kinship obligations, and will be under the scrutiny of lineage or kindred co-members. A father who cannot control a wayward son or wife can get help from co-members. Thus the forces that tend to turn a family in on itself, concerned only with its own problems, are partly countervailed by the demands of the larger kinship structure.

However, it is then understandable that when a society becomes urbanized or industrialized, the clan, lineage, kindred, or other descent grouping weakens and decays. All these activities can be performed by impersonal, non-kinship agencies, whether governmental or private. A lineage need not protect an individual family, if an adequate police system exists. Close kin remain a major source of small loans even in an industrialized society, but banks become the source of investment capital. In the early stages of industrial transition, a family that commands an effective kinship structure can often forge ahead of families trying to rise on their own. Nevertheless, such structures begin to disappear under industrialization. Even in societies where they existed for centuries before the modern era they were much weaker in cities than in outlying rural areas.

Matrilineage

Perhaps the best way to understand this type of descent grouping is to look at one kind, and it is useful to consider a type which is far removed from our ordinary experience. Here we shall simply trace out the consequences of a matrilineage for a range of kinship role relationships,[2] and by contrast see more clearly the traits of a patrilineage. One caution applies here, as in all analyses of descent groups. In no society is the sole emphasis on a single descent line. In all patrilineages, for example, many rights and obligations tie an individual to his mother's kinship line. Moreover, the frequency of social contact based on common residence often outweighs the day-to-day importance of lineage ties. Families that live close to one another may call upon one another for help far more than they call on co-members of their lineage.

The essential structure of matrilineage can be described simply—an individual is part of a descent group whose members are linked *through* the successive generations of females. A boy and his sister are members of their mother's lineage, and she and her brothers and sisters are part of *their* mother's lineage. Since no society is a matriarchy, every lineage contains men, who will hold the most important positions. At the same time, since almost every individual eventually marries, the lineage is composed of both men and women who are *married to non-members*. This situation results from the fact that members are linked by descent, but lineages are exogamous. Everyone marries outside the lineage, but everyone in the society is a member of *some* lineage. A given matrilineage, then, excludes the women who are married to the men in it, as well as the men who have married its female members. Naturally, then, the lineage is never a *residential* kinship group. Its members are found in many families, some of whose members are part of one lineage, and the rest of whom are part of another lineage.

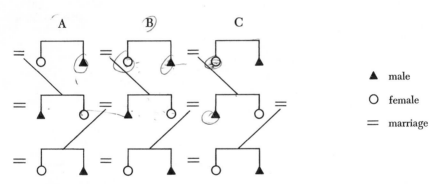

Figure 1. *Patrilateral cross-cousin marriage in a matrilineal system.* From George C. Homans and David M. Schneider, *Marriage, Authority, and Final Causes* (Glencoe, Ill.: The Free Press, 1955), p. 11.

In Fig. 1, the connections of one generation with another can be seen. A, B, and C are three matrilineages, each exchanging wives and husbands with one another through the common pattern of patrilineal cross-cousin marriage (a man marrying his father's sister's daughter). A more complete but very complex diagram would show all the members of the lineage within a given society —i.e., including the collateral relatives who are part of the same lineage.

Notice from the diagram that in a matrilineage, when a man marries he

[2] This section is based on David M. Schneider, "The Distinctive Features of Matrilineal Descent Groups," in David M. Schneider and Kathleen Gough (eds.), *Matrilineal Kinship* (Berkeley: University of California Press, 1961), pp. 1–29.

does not produce children for his matrilineage. They belong to his wife's lineage. His sister, however, marries and produces children for *his* matrilineage. Although members of a lineage produce children, as it were, for other lineages, over time the exchanges balance out. Since each lineage depends on others, the society is more closely integrated.

Although a matrilineage is sometimes described as the mirror image of a patrilineage, close study of the relevant descent charts discloses important structural differences. The first lies in the fact that the matrilineage must restrain and control the in-marrying males, who by the status definitions of the society will have considerable authority, as husbands and as males. In a patrilineage, on the other hand, there are no in-marrying males, and the in-marrying females can be controlled simply because all members of the society agree they should be subordinate. In some patrilineages the wives are assimilated to a considerable degree into their husband's lineage, but even if they are not, they form no threat. They produce no sons for their own lineage, and cannot assume authority in their own right.

Because mother's brother is an authority figure—the representative of the family in ritual matters, and the man from whom a boy (brother's sister's son) inherits—these two statuses are closely linked but in a different way from that of the patrilineage. In the latter a father is *both* an authority figure and a source of tenderness. In a matrilineage a father can be a source of tenderness (like a mother's brother in our society), but his authority must be limited at certain points by the lineage. Indeed, since his property goes to *his* sister's sons, and he must spend a great deal of time with them as they become older, he has less grounds for demanding obedience from his own sons. On the other hand, because he loves his sons, works with them, and interacts with them daily, one type of additional strain is evident. He may wish to help them, to offer them gifts, or even to bequeath some possessions to them, to the annoyance of his nephews specifically and his lineage generally.

Since the position of the in-marrying male is under some strain, and the rights and duties of the wife with reference to *domestic* affairs (where she is clearly under his authority) must be closely defined, the divorce rate is likely to be high in a matrilineal system. The children remain with the woman, since they belong to her lineage. In some types of conflicts with her husband, she can obtain support from her kinsmen, and especially from her brothers. The available data confirm this prediction. In general, strong, durable, intense links between husband and wife are less common in matrilineages than in patrilineages.

One consequence of this is that the bride price in a matrilineal system is likely to be low. The elders of a family or a lineage will not invest much in a union that is not likely to endure, and besides, the lineage of the *male* does not receive children from the union. A patrilineage, on the other hand, not only will receive the services of the in-marrying woman but also the children she bears. Moreover, the woman gets less support from her kin, in the event of a domestic quarrel, so that divorce is less likely. Thus the bride price is likely to be more substantial in a patrilineage.

Matrilineal systems can be found in many parts of the world, but make up only about 15 per cent of the world's societies. A great belt of matrilineal tribes runs from West Africa eastward across the continent. The Navaho and Zuñi of the Southwestern U.S. are also matrilineal, and the sub-continent of India once contained many matrilineal groups, of which the best described are the Nayars, who reside along the Malabar Coast. Some are also found in Melanesia in the South Pacific. One of these tribes, the Trobrianders, is

organized descent groupings

analyzed in the classic field work of Bronislaw Malinowski. Clearly, they are not found in the least industrialized societies. Nor are they prevalent among societies that are highly advanced in technology. Matriliny seems not to be, as once was thought, the "primeval" kinship pattern, created before human beings learned of the connection between sexual intercourse and birth. Matriliny is most likely to be found in societies which engage in gardening but do not use the plow (in horticultural societies) and in which women thus play an important role in food production. In societies which demand large-scale co-operation among males, or which assign central societal tasks to political or economic organizations *not* based on kinship, matrilineages are nearly absent.

The Chinese Clan

The Chinese clan system was most fully developed in the southeast provinces, such as Fukien, Kwantung, Kwangsi, and Kiangsi, but the general pattern shaped much of family life throughout China. This system continued until 1949, when the Communist regime assumed power, although it had already gradually declined in significance in the cities, toward the northwest, and of course in the spreading areas under Communist control from the 1930's on.

To the Westerner it was symbolized most dramatically by the considerable number of villages, in both southern and northern China, in which almost everyone had the same surname. From the administrative point of view, its significance may be seen in the fact that under the Empire the administrative apparatus did not reach down to the village level, where the strength of the clan typically maintained peace and order.

The large Chinese population has shared about 500 surnames, many of which were uncommon. This did not mean, of course, that everyone with the same surname was involved in *clan* relations with one another; but the vague feeling of kinship was strong enough to support a strong rule that people of the same name should not marry. In addition, having the same surname did make introductions or voluntary associations easier between strangers, especially in areas distant from their birthplace. In general, those with the same surname were supposed to be helpful to one another.

The formally organized operative descent group was, however, localized, confined to one area in a town, or to a single village. Since such a clan might well have been settled in the area for 10 to 20 generations, other sub-clans descended from the same supposed ancestor might well dominate other nearby localities, villages, or parts of towns. These sub-branches would not meet together as a unitary whole, but would know that they were descended from the same ancestor, and would probably even recognize which group was the senior or main branch, as well as the order of seniority of the sub-branches in the clan. Each village clan maintained, or felt an obligation to maintain, a clan temple in which the ancestral tablets were kept, refurbished, and displayed. If sufficiently prosperous, the clan might have common land, used to pay for the upkeep of the temple or for other clan activities. This land would be rented to clan members, under various sets of rules, though usually it was the more powerful families within the clan who succeeded in controlling the land.

A village could be dominated by one clan numerically. All the wives had to be non-members of the clan, and therefore came from nearby villages. In addition, an outsider might—because of the familistic loyalties of the Chinese—have some difficulty in political or economic competition with members of the organization. However, larger villages or towns would have more than one clan, and these vied with one another for prestige and honor. If a clan became

organized descent groupings

prosperous, it might hire a scholar to "research" its history in order to prove its illustrious origins and history. At a death or marriage, the clan members would contribute to the ceremony in order to display their wealth or past achievements. Since the Chinese government carried out so few tasks at the village level, a wide range of activities was the responsibility of clans, from building a hospital to ridding an area of bandits.

In addition, some clans attempted to pay for schools, since the most prestige would accrue to the clan who produced learned scholars, especially those who rose to high position in the Imperial bureaucracy. The clan also served at times as a parole body for a man who had disobeyed the law but who had reformed. Its importance was recognized in the rule that a man should not be an Imperial governor in his own province, because he could not dispense justice to all impartially. Nepotism was both expected and approved in Chinese society, and this rule at least reduced the temptation.

The head of a local clan was, ideally, the oldest member, but in fact education, power, and wealth counted for more in the actual clan decisions. A clan might have a council of elders, but perhaps most did not. In any event, seniority was respected, primarily in a symbolic fashion if an older man did not have other qualities that commanded assent.

The clan did not interfere in the domestic affairs of the family. Its importance lay outside the household, unless the male head could not maintain his authority. Precisely because the clan could concentrate both economic and political power, it was a significant resource to be exploited. Since individual poor families could not, except in unusual situations, call on governmental agencies for help, they were not able to escape or to resist clan influence. Where the clan owned agricultural land, it was supposed to be rotated among families according to clan rules, but the stronger families were more likely to use this land when they wished. If taxes were to be collected, the rich could pay less than they should.

In the cities the poor families could more easily escape clan influence, and could obtain all its main benefits from other agencies. The rich urban families did not wish to recognize their vague obligation to help their kinsmen. After the 1911 Revolution which destroyed the Manchu Dynasty, the Republic created new political authorities in the villages, elected by the people. These did not fully replace the clans, but they were sometimes a force to be reckoned with. By the 1930's the clan seems to have become weaker in even those areas where it had once been strong.

As already mentioned, in Imperial China, and to some extent under the Republic, the rule of the central government extended only partially to affairs at the village level. By contrast, the power of the clan was local. It was for this reason that the Communists aimed at destroying the clan, since they intended to control as much of Chinese life as possible. The clan was viewed as the locus of old superstitions and "feudal practices." It was a possible source of countervailing political authority. The Communists also saw it as the tool of the rich, and as an instrument of a corrupt regime.

Therefore, they moved to eradicate the clan from Chinese life. Economic life was to be directed by the state, not the clan. Populations have been moved about a good deal, in order to sever the clan ties that were essentially localized. Where ancestral graves, groves, and halls existed, they were taken over. Where clan agricultural land existed, it was expropriated. Over the decade between 1949 and 1959, the Chinese supplanted the clan by their own corporate—but non-kinship—agency, the commune system.

The "core" of the Chinese clan was close to the ideal, symmetrical network of "mourning relatives" or mourning grades—i.e., the most important people for the purposes of mourning. These were (1) a man's direct male *ascendants* through his great-great-grandfather; (2) a man's lineal descendants through his great-great-grandson, and (3) the collateral relatives four degrees from the man at his own generation, three from his father and son, two from his grandfather and grandson, and one from his great-grandfather and great-grandson. In and of itself, this was not a corporate group, since obviously its limits would differ for different individuals. A full chart would also include all the obligations for mothers, who did not really become part of their husband's clan until the women died. Obviously, only a rare man would have great-great-grandsons, and if he did all his ancestors would be dead. Thus, the chart would tell us more about where respect was to be paid in the direct family line, than who was administering the local clan. It would pay less attention to the juniors, but under the old system these would in turn eventually become adult, to be reckoned with in the day-to-day affairs of the village clan. It emphasized the main line of adult males, which remains the prime focus of family loyalty now, when the clan itself has nearly disappeared.

The Japanese *Dozoku*

The Japanese, like other nations, did not typically live in extended households. In late Tokugawa times, about half of Japanese households were nuclear in fact, and even about 40 years ago some three-fifths of all Japanese lived in nuclear families. But as mentioned earlier, the Japanese family was a "stem" family. One person inherited the headship of the family and thus represented the continuation of the family line. This person, usually the oldest in upper-class families, took some responsibility for the younger siblings. It was expected that younger brothers would not remain in the household, and indeed Japanese folklore asserted that younger brothers were more likely to be daring and original than the oldest brother, since the young ones were pushed out to live on their own. The oldest son was a kind of trustee for the "line," however, and was responsible for maintaining its prestige and honor.

If economic conditions were ideal, a younger brother might found a branch or junior family line. Both the senior and the junior families, it must be emphasized, represented a link in the unbroken chain of the family, and did not form a clan composed of many *collateral* kin. In rural areas, however, and among upper-class urban strata, a senior line might well link with one or more junior branches to form a *dozoku*. The link had deep roots in the Japanese family tradition. A "household" was not simply where a family lived, or even an aggregate of the living members. It was the repository of all the history of that family line, paying reverence to its dead members and maintaining, within the limits of its space and budget, mementos of the past. A wife was usually not inscribed in the family register until she had borne a child, preferably a son. Thus a junior household was not simply a group of kin, but a bearer of the family honor, and shared that responsibility with the senior branch.

In any given *dozoku* there was only one *honke*, or senior branch. If economic and social opportunities had been favorable in the past, and the family had taken advantage of them, there might be one or more junior branches of varying historical depth. These people, with their wives, formed the nucleus of blood kin within the center of the *dozoku*. In some regions no other people were part of the kinship unit.

In many areas other families were included in this grouping. For the most part, the larger organization was found in forestry and fishing villages.

64

Such families did not inherit their positions without question, but had to validate them by working for the core families in the *dozoku*. Their status was not quite that of serfs, but then this was not a free market. Only certain families would be given the opportunity to work for the higher ranking core members of the clan. The non-consanguineous families did not inherit land or authority, and their duties and rights were defined by tradition. The links among these families were reaffirmed on ritual occasions, such as the Buddhist All Soul's Day.[3]

Japanese society was feudal, and the feudal relationship of patron-protegé, lord and master, extended into family relations as well. These "ritual kin" gave their labor and loyalty to the core families in the *dozoku*, and in turn received some economic and physical security. The system had the approval of the Imperial government, since thereby the less advantaged social strata were held in place by a network of obligations and duties, and could be no threat to national order. This hierarchical system was also the model of a widespread social pattern in Japan, by which many individuals recognized others as patrons, as a major source of present, past, and future benefits, to whom the protegés paid deference, loyalty, and service in turn. This *oyabun-kobun* relationship was found in cities as well as rural areas, and in all occupational areas, but was more personalized and individual than the relations among members of the *dozoku*.

As in China, the Japanese "clan" was of less importance in the cities, for without a landed base the family could not easily hold together both its members and its subordinates. The services obtained from subordinates could as easily be bought. However, an individual patron or *oyabun* might be needed by even an urban family of some standing because of new goals it wished to realize. The family might wish to enroll a son in the Imperial university, or obtain a job for him in a bank (i.e., essentially new urban aspirations), and for this might need the support of a highly placed person.

This more individual patron-protegé relationship still continues in Japan in the traditional arts, in the form of the master-apprentice link, and in academic life. By the Meiji period (1868–1912), the senior and junior branches of the *dozoku* had ceased to cooperate in vital matters, and acted independently of one another.[4] In rural areas this type of clan had lost its base by the end of World War II. Before that time, the power of a few families over the land had very likely been increasing: In 1892, 40 per cent of Japanese farmers were tenants, and by 1945, the figure had risen to 60 per cent. The land reforms under the Allied occupation reduced tenancy to the point where between 80 to 90 per cent were either owners, or owners in addition to being tenants. Thus neither the individual nor his family depended primarily on the *dozoku* for land, and of course the expansion of industry opened alternative opportunities for young men. Within the modern world, the *dozoku* also remains of importance among some of the Japanese families who direct great commercial and industrial corporations.

The Kindred

Since the kindred is likely to include blood kin in all directions, and is a residential unit as well (to include many affinals), its bound-

[3] Further details on this type of kin grouping can be found in Kizaemon Ariga, *Dozoku* (Columbus, Ohio: Office of Naval Research Project, NR 176–110 and Rockefeller Foundation, Interim Technical Report No. 7, September 1953).

[4] Kunio Yanagida, *Japanese Manners and Customs in the Meiji Era*, translated by C.S. Terry (Tokyo: Obunsha, 1957), p. 104.

aries are much less clear than those of a lineage or clan. Its boundaries differ for every one of its members. An individual's mother's brother will be in it, but if he counts as co-members everyone within, say, five degrees of kinship, he will include some people who are more distant from the mother's brother than five degrees. Kindreds were found in the rural U.S. in the nineteenth century, but have not been genuine corporate bodies in the West since the beginning of the Middle Ages. Murdock found them in 30 per cent of his sample, as against some 65 per cent with lineages, but he argues that they are probably even more frequent than this figure suggests.[5]

This form of descent grouping was found among the early Indo-European and Semitic tribes, and persists today among some of the Polynesians and a few other tribes in various parts of the world. Notice that it is *not* exogamous, but endogamous. It contains many people, so that it is likely to contain a potential spouse. (In general, the smaller the kinship group, the more likely it is to be exogamous.) By contrast, an individual can marry a very close "relative" in a unilineage system, since he has only to move outside his own lineage to find people with similar cultural patterns, nearby and linked by at least affinal ties with him. In a kindred he may also marry a parallel cousin (e.g., father's brother's daughter). The central core of the kindred very likely will be the dominant families who bear the name of the kindred.

Since those who are closest to the main line of descent are viewed as the carriers of the traditions of the kindred, much attention is paid to genealogies. These must be charted with great care because so many families must be included, whereas in a lineage only the single line need be reckoned. The kindred, however, does not have as clear boundaries as a lineage, and thus in a conflict or even in the matter of property ownership it cannot function so effectively. Because everyone is in a different position in the total unit, and its boundaries extend indefinitely in all directions, people in it may be in conflict, with one another, but call on a different set of relatives for support. Thus internal conflict is possible; and in an external conflict, mustering everyone is not easy, since those distant from the core kin do not feel the same definite sense of membership and may feel just as close to another kindred. It is as though the "McCoys" of ballad fame were fighting with the Hatfields, but at many points they would be linked by many kinship ties, making it difficult to mount a joint battle. A man's duties in a unilineage are clear, however, because his membership is clear.

This means, more generally, that kindreds cannot be clear segments of a society, and cannot easily act as a collectivity, either in owning land or administering political justice. On the other hand, they can achieve local control over their constituent families within a delimited area, and some believe that their core of dominant families becomes, over time, the aristocratic stratum of a somewhat more complex, stratified society.

[5] George P. Murdock, *Social Structure* (New York: Macmillan, 1949), p. 57.

organized descent groupings

role relations
of spouses
and parents
in family
and society

seven

The statuses of spouses and parents are fixed by obligations within the family as well as in the larger society. In assigning certain jobs to men outside the household, society determines in part the division of labor *internal* to the family, just as what work children and parents perform within the family shapes what tasks will be given to them outside the family. Parents have the responsibility of initially socializing their children, but also thereby of maintaining social control over them when they are away from the household.

In this chapter, then, we shall consider especially those role relations internal to the family that reflect the position of family members in the outside society. We shall point up age and sex differences as they are shown in the family division of labor and in authority patterns, and the relations of parents to children in the socializing process.

Since the status of the individual, and thus his social relations, will change in many ways throughout his own life cycle and that of his two families (of birth and parenthood), it is useful to consider first some descriptive facts about the life cycle of the family in the U.S., as it goes through the stages of formation, growth, and dissolution by death or divorce.

Life Cycle of the Family

At first marriage, in the U.S., the husband is about 22 years of age and his wife is about 20.[1] In the intact family the wife will bear her first child within about one and one-half years after the marriage. Adequate data on child-spacing are scarce. In one study 45 per cent of women in the 1950's who were 30 to 34 years of age and who had 3 live children had their first child within the first year of marriage. Of course, these were among the more fertile mothers. Their second child came about 2½ years later, and the third, approximately 3 years after that.

Of course, such a fertile sample does not yield precise data for all groups of the population. Young women in this generation are bearing about 2.8 children during their lifetimes, and have completed their childbearing, on the average, by the time they are in their 26th or 27th year. This is about 6 years younger than were their grandmothers at the same phase in the life cycle of their families.

Most young people attempt to set up their own households at marriage. In the 1950's, after the postwar housing shortage had eased somewhat, only about 1 wife out of 8 under 25 years of age was without a household of her own. It is young couples who are more likely to live with one or the other set of parents for a while. Aside from age, regional differences exist: Doubling up is more common in the South than in other regions of the United States.

Most women work outside the home at some time in their lives, but at any given time a majority is outside the labor force. The peak of participation is just before marriage, when about half are working. About 1 out of 5 women with pre-school children has an outside job. Women in their thirties are likely to return to work—i.e., after all the children are in school (at about age 32)—but in the late forties the curve drops off and continues downward from that point on.

Divorce may happen at any time in the life cycle of the family. The median age at divorce is about 30 years, about 2 years older than the age at separation. Most marriages, however, do endure until the death of the husband or wife. By the time the last child has left home, the parents are close to 50 years of age. At current mortality rates, this means they have lived through two-thirds of their married life. Because women have lower mortality rates, and are usually younger than their husbands, they are likely to become widows. After the last child marries, the wife can expect (if she is the survivor) to live for about twenty-five years.

Role relations change not only at such clear points as these, but continually, throughout the life of the family. The infant begins his life well-protected, but within a few years he must face unrelenting demands from his parents, his siblings, and his playmates. Each person is gradually shaped by everyone else in the family.

Since each person is different in some ways, and since rights and duties are somewhat different in each family, the structure of role interaction also varies from one home to another. Within these changes and idiosyncrasies, however, are many regularities. Though parental duties alter with the age and number of children, they do so only within broad limits, characteristic of a given society. Appropriate behavior in a female varies as she shifts her attention from dolls to boy friends, and from her babies to her married children;

---

[1] The figures in this section are largely drawn from Paul C. Glick, *American Families* (New York: Wiley, 1957), Chaps. 3–5.

68

but both society and family continue to demand that she fit feminine role models.

These pressures begin with the earliest socialization experience and continue throughout life. There is considerable uniformity among societies with reference to many role demands, especially to those which define feminine and masculine behavior. One study investigated to what extent societies are likely to demand different kinds of behavior from boys and girls. Most reports describe the adult sexual division of labor, and some differences in the behavior of boys and girls, but do not systematically record whether the people in a given society demand more nurturance, obedience, responsibility, achievement, or self-reliance from boys than from girls. In four-fifths of nearly 100 societies for which information was available, the socialization of girls emphasized nurturance more than that of boys. In three-fifths, girls were pressed toward responsibility ("being dutiful") more than were boys.[2] In about one-third of these cultures, girls were urged to obedience more than were boys, but in the remainder no substantial difference could be observed. Finally, in more than four-fifths of these societies (85 to 87%) boys were more strongly pushed toward achievement and self-reliance than were girls. The reader may usefully compare these findings with his experiences in his own culture.

How *successfully* the family achieves the goal of inculcating appropriate sex roles depends in part on family structure, especially whether adequate role models are available. A boy reared with older brothers is more likely to accept fully the masculine traits of his culture than is a boy reared with older sisters only. Research data suggest that in a family containing only two children, a boy and a girl, each will assimilate somewhat the traits of the opposite sex. If the father is absent for much of the time, boys and girls will differ somewhat from the usual sex patterns. In one study of father absence in sailor families, in a region where this type of absence is socially normal, it was ascertained that boys whose fathers are absent for long periods are likely to have a poorer adjustment with their age mates than a control group of boys, whereas this difference was not found among girls.[3] The mother is less likely to work outside the home and is more likely to overprotect her children. There is some evidence of role conflict in such boys, for they are less likely to be aggressive in play, but more likely to engage in fantasies of strongly masculine behavior, or to exhibit an exaggerated but surface masculinity. Having insufficient direct experience with the appropriate father model, both girls and boys are likely to vary somewhat from the socially expected, sex-linked patterns of conduct and personality.

Sexual Division of Labor

These early socialization experiences in which youngsters begin to acquire the values and skills of their parents are the foundations for their later adult behavior, when they become parents and spouses. The differences in sex roles appear strikingly in the sexual division of labor. In all societies a range of tasks is assigned to women and another set of tasks given

[2] Herbert Barry, Margaret K. Bacon, and Irvin L. Child, "A Cross-Cultural Survey of Some Sex Differences in Socialization," in Robert F. Winch, Robert McGinnis, and Herbert R. Barringer (eds.), *Selected Studies in Marriage and the Family* (New York: Holt, Rinehart, and Winston, 1962), p. 269.

[3] Per Olav Tiller, "Father Absence and Personality Development of Children in Sailor Families. A Preliminary Research Report," in Nels Anderson (ed.), *Recherches sur la Famille* (Göttingen: Vandenhoeck and Ruprecht, 1957), pp. 115–133.

to men, and still others may be performed by either sex. Very little of this division is required by the biological peculiarities of the two sexes. A man cannot bear a child or nurse it. Men are stronger and can run faster than women, who are in turn somewhat handicapped at times by pregnancy and menstruation. Women however, have enough strength and speed to perform almost all tasks in every society. Equally important, what is defined as a man's task in one society may well be classed as a woman's job in another, thus indicating that most of the division is culturally defined, or based on a complex of factors in which the biological is only a part. However, in three-fourths or more of societies for which information is available, women carry out these tasks; grinding grain, carrying water, cooking, preserving food, repairing and making clothing, weaving (of cloth, mats, and baskets), gathering food (nuts, berries, herbs, roots, etc.), and making pottery.[4] All these tasks can be carried out while remaining close to the children or the hearth.

In most societies men are assigned these tasks: herding, hunting and fishing, lumbering, mining and quarrying, metal-working, making musical instruments, manufacturing ceremonial objects, wood-working, and house-building. Some of these require strength, and others demand some wandering from the hearth. Others demand neither strength nor absence from the home. Notice that the tending of crops calls for endurance and some strength, but it is as likely to be a female activity as a male activity.

That the division is not based on a rational judgment of capacity is seen from the fact that men can in fact perform all the women's jobs, but do not, whereas the jobs that are strictly male do not generally take all the man's time. The division of labor is based neither on biology nor on simple equality. Another factor is significant, as an element in the husband's position, and the position of men in the society: Whatever the strictly male tasks are, they are defined as *more honorific*.

This element suggests that the sexual division of labor, within family and society, comes perilously close to the racial or caste restrictions in some modern countries. That is, the low-ranking race, caste, or sex is defined as not being *able* to do certain types of prestigious work, but it is also considered a violation of propriety if they do it. Obviously, if women really cannot do various kinds of male tasks, no moral or ethical prohibition would be necessary to keep them from it.

It is safe to say, even without a complete tabulation, that in no society are men and women free to choose whatever tasks they want, using the criteria of efficiency, convenience, and capacity. There is not a "free labor market" in this matter. Moreover, the tasks of control, management, decision, appeals to the gods—in short, the higher level jobs that typically do *not* require strength, speed, or traveling far from home—are male jobs. In primitive or highly industrialized societies, men object to women taking over high level jobs, and object themselves to taking over women's tasks. This is true in Communist China and to some extent in the Israeli *kibbutzim*, just as it is in the United States, though women in fact have been given important jobs in all three. The division is justified by various rationalizations and by moral precepts, and these are part of the socialization experience of boys and girls in the society. From the beginning, the boy learns to disdain some work as female, and to aspire to other tasks as masculine.

4 George P. Murdock, *Social Structure* (New York: Macmillan, 1949), p. 213.

role relations of spouses and parents in family and society

Sex Roles

The parallel between jobs and the major role obligations of father and mother within the family is clear. The mother begins with the nurturance of the child, establishing a close physical and psychological bond because of the gratifications both give one another. Her social *relational* tasks are expressive, emotional, or integrative. She is to console, to nurse, to bring together again those who have quarreled. The father is the instrumental leader, organizing family labor for production, political conflicts, or war. He must solve the problems of the outside environment, social or physical. Because of this division of social labor, a family that has a weak or ineffectual mother, or a cold, unyielding father, is less likely to fail in its socializing tasks than one in which there is either a cold, unyielding mother or a weak, ineffectual father.[5] This allocation of social tasks exists in most societies.

We might mention here other differences in social position with the family. One is that as against the variations among societies in their disapproval of premarital or extramarital sexual intercourse, perhaps all agree in never placing more severe restrictions on men than on women.[6] Usually, of course, as in the Western countries, the restrictions on women are much stronger.

Occupying different statuses and rank and dealing with different types of tasks, men and women necessarily live in some tension with one another, especially when they both approach the same problem with discrepant orientations. The supposed differences between men and women in their ways of thinking have been the subject of many essays. One such intuitive commentary was drawn from contemporary research in a Canadian community. Without asserting that the list is correct, let us look at a few such divergences in orientation.[7]

The researchers note first that women deny or play down any great differences between men and women, but men not only take the differences for granted but also believe women to be so sentimental and non-logical that they are not even capable of seeing the differences. Next, women stress the unique qualities of people, especially of their children, and view social institutions, laws, and other general patterns as obstacles to helping individuals. In action however, both men and women contradict their values. Men believe in the greater value of *collectivity*, but they work for it through the fine adjustments or manipulations of *individuals*; and they, too, see norms, laws, and universalistic rules as obstacles to be by-passed in the interest of their individual companies.

Also, women are said to be determinists, especially psychological determinists; men, on the other hand, assert that individuals are free, that the man who *wants* to do something can do it. There is a paradox in women's faith in perfectibility, a belief that people can be made indefinitely better. Men dismiss such a view as naïve. However, women are more likely to adjust to

---

[5] The terms "instrumental" and "expressive" are from Morris Zelditch, "Role Differentiation in the Nuclear Family: A Comparative Study," in Talcott Parsons and Robert F. Bales (eds.), *Family, Socialization and Interaction Process* (Glencoe, Ill.: The Free Press, 1955), pp. 307–351.

[6] William N. Stephens, *The Family in Cross-Cultural Perspective* (New York: Holt, Rinehart and Winston, 1963), pp. 290 ff.

[7] John R. Seeley, R. Alexander Sim, and Elizabeth W. Loosley, "Differentiation of Values in a Modern Community," in Norman W. Bell and Ezra W. F. Vogel (eds.), *The Family* (Glencoe, Ill.: The Free Press, 1960), pp. 453–464. The section is taken from *Crestwood Heights*.

the apparent intractabilities and inflexibilities in others, whereas men are more likely to insist on continuous improvement.

Whether the different socialization experiences and social positions of men and women actually lead to such striking qualitative contrasts in action and attitude seems unlikely, but the technical problems of inquiry into these points are well worth studying.

Marital Adjustment

The relations between husband and wife are discussed at many points in this book. However, brief attention should also be paid to marital adjustment itself, a subject which is at once of great personal interest and the object of considerable objective research. For the past generation, sociologists and psychologists have tried to define and "measure" marital happiness and to ascertain which characteristics might best assure this blessed state. The most sophisticated work has been done under the influence of Ernest W. Burgess, and some variation of his and Leonard S. Cottrell's marital adjustment scale has been used in many studies and on a wide range of populations. The researchers have developed this instrument by finding which background traits (age at marriage, religious affiliation, length of engagement, etc.) and which current patterns (community of interests, expression of affection, etc.) are associated with marital satisfaction. Those items which exhibited no correlation with adjustment were discarded. Widely used by marital counselors and by teachers of courses in marriage, the marital adjustment questionnaire has been used as a basis for persuading people to delay marriage, as a point of departure for interviewing, and as a diagnostic tool for locating problem areas in an engagement or marriage.[8] If indeed we can now predict at least which *kinds* of people have the highest chances of marital happiness, or which types of couples are poorer risks, then we might be more rational in ordering our lives. And, of course, the use of such prediction instruments is no more than a formalized or impersonal way of making the kinds of predictions that kin and friends always make when a couple plans to marry.

Some critics have argued that it is not possible to "measure" marital adjustment, and doubtless what some call "reasonably contented" others might call miserable. However, how we feel at any given moment we are asked about is no secret to ourselves. We may report incorrectly to others, but few persons will tell themselves they are happy in marriage when they are not. In Western societies, and especially in the United States, far more people seem to be actively *seeking* marital happiness, and to be concerned about it, than in most societies of the past. In only some societies have marriages been arranged mainly for the personal happiness of the husband and wife. Instead, their greater concern, like that of their kin, was whether each did his or her duty and paid each other proper respect. This was easier to do when the role relations were more clearly specified by the larger society, and there was greater agreement among its members on these duties and rights—and thus steadier pressure on everyone to conform.

The discriminating power of the marital adjustment prediction questionnaire has, however, never been impressive. It would be wrong to say that its power is no greater than that of common sense, for one clear result of these researches is that few of the inituitive "truths" about who should marry whom

---

[8] The two most sophisticated studies in this area are by Harvey J. Locke, *Predicting Adjustment in Marriage* (New York: Holt, 1951); and Ernest W. Burgess and Paul W. Wallin, *Engagement and Marriage* (New York: Lippincott, 1953). See also the criticisms by Clifford Kirkpatrick, *The Family* (New York: Ronald, 1955), pp. 340 ff.

role relations of spouses and parents in family and society

are secure enough to be trusted as guides. The most general point is that individuals who have very "traditional" backgrounds are more likely to be contented in marriage—or are more likely, at least, to *say* they are contented. Thus if the individual himself comes from a contented family and had a long acquaintanceship and engagement with his wife, his marriage seems to be a better risk. Data from other sources, and common sense, too, suggest that a similar background is more likely to lead to marital contentment, but a moment's thought (or the prediction instrument data) will remind us that people who share an interest in hanging around bars and taxi dance halls, or have a common background of divorce, are not likely to create enduring or contented marriages. The prediction instrument also suggests that common sense is wrong in supposing that a satisfactory sexual adjustment is the most important foundation of a secure marriage. Instead, as marital counselors have pointed out for nearly two decades, it is very likely a secure marriage that creates or fosters a sound sexual adjustment.

Unfortunately, not one major factor has been confirmed by all researchers as being highly correlated with marital happiness, and those factors which seem of some importance discriminate only grossly between traditional couples and the rest of the population (e.g., having parents whose marriage was happy, being acquainted and engaged for a long time, husband's close attachment to father). Without finer discrimination, the prediction questionnaire can offer little in the way of sound guidance, although counselors have used it widely. Perhaps a new direction of research, which would focus only on marital stability, and the profiles or fit between bride and groom, is now in order.

Husband-Wife Bonds and the Social Network

The relationship between husband and wife is shaped by the network of friends and kin in which they live. In the major civilizations of the past, it is likely that the kinship network was most important. But though friends may substitute for kin in the modern social network to some extent, certain *general* relations between husband and wife seem to be caused by the nature of the *network* itself. This may be seen more clearly in tentative results from recent research in England, on the relatedness of these networks [9]—i.e., the extent to which the friends of the husband or wife are *also* friends of one another.

First, it seems clear that most families in the West now live in social networks rather than in *groups*. That is, they are not part of a social unit having clear physical or social boundaries, sharing certain norms, and having some clear identity. Rather, one family is in social interaction with a large or small number of other families, each of which may have (1) interaction with one or more other families in that number, plus (2) interaction with still *other* families. Thus, starting from any given family, the network extends indefinitely in any direction, with much overlapping of interaction, frequency of contact, and intimacy in any area of the network; but always there are some families who are linked together only because they have acquaintances in common, but who have little contact with one another.

Second, the *tightness* of the connections among the families in any family's network may be high or low. A family lives in a closely knit network if the family units see one another frequently, *independently of that family*. It is loosely knit if they do not interact with one another frequently.

Husbands and wives whose network is closely knit are likely to share a

[9] Elizabeth Bott, *Family and Social Network* (London: Tavistock Publications, 1957), pp. 52 ff., 92 ff.

role relations of spouses and parents in family and society

somewhat different life pattern than do couples in a loosely knit network. The former will spend more time apart. The husband sees his friends independently of his wife. They divide the household responsibilities more sharply: The husband does not do "women's work," nor does the wife take on her husband's duties as much as do other wives. In short, in a tightly knit network, the husband and wife engage in complementary but independent activities. In a loosely knit network the husband and wife are more likely to share each other's domestic tasks and to go about together for recreation or visiting.

This important difference may be partly related to class position, since the loosely knit network seems to be found more often in professional families. It may also be related to homogeneity and stability of neighborhood, since the tightly knit network is more likely to be found in such areas. Perhaps a more central factor is the couple's dependence on this network of friends and kin prior to their marriage. When individuals have lived in a tightly knit network prior to their marriage, and have remained in the same area, they are likely to obtain both emotional satisfaction and services from it afterward.

Husband and wife can more easily keep their activities segregated if they are in a tightly knit network, since mutual help is more available in the network itself. Joint organization of tasks is more necessary, the less a couple can count on an outside network for help. Moreover, to the extent that they have outside resources, neither husband nor wife needs to invest so much emotion in their own domestic tie; of course, the outside relations may at times interfere with the solidarity of the husband-wife unit.

This contrast parallels a contrast made earlier, between the modern conjugal family, less dependent on its kin network, and the nuclear or polygynous family embedded within a large controlling kin group in most primitive or peasant societies. In the latter, the husband-wife tie is less close, their tasks are more segregated, and they are more likely to see their friends separately rather than as a couple. Moreover, these comments apply not only to the husband-wife relation in primitive societies but also to some family units in a modern metropolis, when they are in intimate interaction with a tight kinship network. However, these observations need to be tested by more rigorous research on larger urban populations.

Authority of the Male

Because the increasing privileges of women in the Western World over the past half-century have presumably reduced the authority of men in the household, several studies have attempted to sketch the decline of patriarchal family patterns or to measure how decisions are actually reached within the family. Apparently in all societies the privilege of major decision is in the hands of men. In most, even the gestures of deference and respect mainly flow from women to men, unlike the U.S. custom. In Western countries, where the stereotypical patriarch seems now to be rare, men are nevertheless able to assert their wills successfully in family matters.

Both observation and experimental study, however, reveal many complexities in this general pattern. Reports from France, Germany, and the United States state that there is a correlation between class position and the authority of the male. Here, a paradox is apparent. Toward the lower strata, the husband is more likely to claim authority simply because he is a male, but actually has to concede more authority to his wife. Toward the upper strata, men are less likely to assert the values of patriarchal authority, but in action manage to have more power anyway. On a common-sense basis, it can be seen that these men have more resources by which to have their way. Their wives are less likely

role relations of spouses and parents in family and society

to work, and even if they do work they contribute a smaller percentage of the total family income than would be true in the lower social strata. Their husbands are less dependent on their wifely services, and can more easily purchase these services. Thus the husband's position in role bargaining is stronger.

Another important complexity exists in the *areas* in which men and women have authority. Observers have often noted the formally obsequious behavior of the Chinese or Japanese wife, and the great authority of the male. In both countries however, the wife and mother assumed greater authority with age (as she doubtless does in all societies) after an initial period of subordination as bride. Within the home she was likely to have considerable authority. The man was indeed paid deference, but he did not ordinarily interfere with household decisions. In Western countries men have begun to aid their wives in the menial tasks of homemaking and child care. This is often called a loss of authority, but it can also be viewed as a gain of authority, for now the husband must be conceded a greater voice in these areas.

Differences in *kinds* of authority may also be important. Readers who have observed first- or second-generation immigrant families from Italian, Greek, or Eastern European Jewish backgrounds are likely to have noticed that though the rhetoric of male dominance is common, the middle-aged or elder matriarch is to be found in many homes. The woman seems to be the center of initiative and decision. However, the male head of the family seems to be *conceding* this authority, reserving the right to take it back when he wishes. If he wants to oppose her will, he can do so successfully. That is, a distinction should perhaps be made between day-to-day initiative and direction, and negative authority— the right to prevent others from doing what they want.

Males usually exercise authority over females, and, as just suggested, older people may demand obedience from younger people. However, one interesting variation on this pattern has been noted here and there, the joking or informal relationship between grandparents and grandchildren. Although the reader is familiar with this behavior, it might seem at first surprising, since the older generation is accorded great deference in most societies. The oldest male in India, China, Japan, and the Arab countries has been the head of the kin group, before whom the young were supposed to be humble. In rural areas of the West, too, the grandparent was viewed as the patriarch. In some societies, however, the grandparent and grandchild may in effect form a coalition against the parents, or treat each other with no reserve at all.

The prime differentiating factor seems to be whether the grandparent continues to rule the parent, to be responsible for directing his daily conduct. When the oldest male remains in the household, and at the top of the family hierarchy, then custom does not permit a relaxed, permissive relationship between grandfather and grandchild. The now widespread informality between grandparent and grandchild in the U.S. family system represents a change from the past, when elders had more authority over their adult, married children.

The Working Mother

Women have always worked, but the modern industrial society is the first in which they have had the right to enter the labor market on their own, to obtain jobs and promotions without the help or permission of their men. Among the Western countries, about 30 to 40 per cent of the non-agricultural labor force is made up of women in these countries: Germany, Denmark, Finland, Sweden, Switzerland, France, Great Britain, and the U.S.— predominantly, the more industrialized countries.

Although in most countries this percentage has not changed greatly over

role relations of spouses and parents in family and society

the past half-century, some qualitative changes are evident. The woman can more easily move into or out of the labor market, and is more fully accepted as a worker. Women have (though in small numbers) been given high posts in every type of work. Very likely, at the turn of the century, few women worked except those who had been driven to it by poverty. Now, far more work to increase substantially the family level of living, or because they want to work.

These and other qualitative changes have given rise to a host of speculations about their consequences for the family. If the wife works, is marital unhappiness or divorce more likely? Are her children more likely to become juvenile delinquents, or to have personality problems? Just how the internal relations among family members are affected when the mother works has not been adequately clarified as yet, but some recent research gives us some preliminary answers, which may be briefly stated here.

First, the employment of mothers increases the frequency of marital conflict, but does not change the general level of happiness in the marriage. This is only a seeming paradox. Offsetting the somewhat greater amount of conflict is presumably a greater amount of satisfaction the woman obtains through the job itself. This inference is supported by the fact that these small differences grow even smaller toward the higher socio-economic strata, where the mother derives more personal satisfaction from the work itself and its attendant rewards.[10]

As might be supposed, the attitude of the husband is relevant here. In families in which the wife works, but the husband disapproves, the level of marital adjustment is lower. However, if the husband approves of his wife working, but she does not work, the level of marital adjustment is *also* lower. If the wife wants to work, but does not, her level of marital adjustment also will be lower.

With reference to the wife's influence in family decisions, present evidence suggests that she gains more power toward the lower socio-economic strata than toward the upper strata when she works. With*in* the area of household tasks, the working wife loses somewhat in authority, since her husband assumes a more important role there. On the other hand, she gains influence in major economic decisions, but neither gains nor loses with respect to control over the husband himself.[11]

No *general* conclusion can be made at present whether working has a destructive effect on the child or relations between mother and children. Class position, the type of work, the age and sex of children, rural-urban residence, and other variables have been shown to interact in complex ways in the final result. Since the family is small, and usually no other adult women live in the household to take care of the children when the mother is absent, obviously the type of surrogate parent available is also of consequence.

A hint of the complexity in such a situation may be noted in the finding that adolescent daughters of middle-class working mothers engage in much organized and unorganized leisure activity. They appear to be more independent, while the amount of family interaction is high. A similar pattern is found among daughters of part-time female workers, whether lower class or middle class. By contrast, the daughters of lower-class working mothers report heavy home responsibilities and fewer leisure activities. They are more likely to seek in steady dating a substitute for a family security or companionship that is lacking.[12]

10 F. Ivan Nye, "Marital Interaction," in F. Ivan Nye and Lois Wladis Hoffman, *The Employed Mother in America* (Chicago: Rand McNally, 1963), pp. 272, 275.
11 Robert O. Blood, "The Husband-Wife Relationship, in *ibid.*, p. 294.
12 Elizabeth Douvan, "Employment and the Adolescent," *ibid.*, pp. 158–159.

role relations of spouses and parents in family and society

The mother who works part-time and the middle-class working mother are both more likely to have *chosen* to work. The former is adjusting her wish to work (or can adjust her need for money) to her family needs. Both these two groups of mothers are likely to choose work they enjoy, and (since they are not so heavily pressed by the sheer need for money) to go into the work with a clear sense of the problems in carrying the double role. Consequently, they feel a greater responsibility for making up for their absence, by better organization, by consciously planning to be with their children, or anticipating and preventing difficulties in their children's life. The lower-class working mother, on the other hand, is more likely to *have to* work, and to have a less pleasant job. She may therefore feel put upon, and be more insistent that her daughters shoulder some of the burden. She feels less need, then, to compensate for her absence, and her daughters are more likely to feel somewhat neglected.

This general interpretation is buttressed somewhat by the fact that the working mother who *likes* to work is more likely to feel a strong attachment to her children, to use only mild discipline, and to avoid shouldering them with household tasks. Her children are less likely to assert themselves against her— but whether or not the mother likes the work, some evidence suggests that young children (third to sixth graders) of working mothers show a lower performance level and are more likely to respond to a frustrating problem with non-adaptive behavior (crying, blaming themselves).[13] Moreover, children of the working mothers who like their work are more likely to show a lower level of *ability*, possibly because these mothers feel the need to compensate for their supposed neglect, and thus over-protect their children, solving their problems for them. Not only levels of ability and performance but an individual's *motivation* to achieve are affected by such variations in internal family relations.

Achievement Motivation

Among the role relations given special attention during the past decade are those that lead to a high need for achievement in boys.[14] Of course, if the society as a whole *outside* the family does not stress achievement, neither will the individuals *within* the family. However, within an achieving society, such as the United States, different groups and social strata vary in their dedication to achievement, and over time a country may move from a high to a low level. Without summarizing the mass of complex and sometimes conflicting evidence, we can point to one or two suggestive findings.

A central thesis is that it is not the warm, indulgent, ever-forgiving mother whose son presses hardest toward achievement, but the mother who consistently demands excellence from him. Nor does the highly successful, dominant father always become the son's role model. Instead, perhaps because the son then comes to feel that he cannot master the environment, cannot master his own destiny, his need for achievement may be lower. If he fails to "win" in the family, he will try less often to win outside it. It is in the family with a wider dispersion of authority, in which the mother has a considerable power, that the achievement-seeking son is more likely to appear. Relative to the importance of this mother-son tie, Freud once wrote of the special grace enjoyed by a boy who knew he was his mother's favorite.

The difference lies not in restrictiveness versus permissiveness. The lower-class boy suffers under more restrictions, and must be more independent than

[13] Lois Wladis Hoffman, "Mothers' Enjoyment of Work and Effects on the Child," *ibid.*, pp. 101–103.

[14] See the body of research reported in David C. McClelland, *The Achieving Society* (New York: D. Van Nostrand, 1961).

the middle- or upper-class boy, who is in turn more likely to be an achiever. Lower-class parents, however, stress that their children be independent so that they will be less of a burden to the parents. The mother of an achieving boy is more likely to tender him emotional support (rewarding achievement with overt affection), to be permissive when it comes to taking care of himself, and also to insist that he make decisions for himself and master certain skills in the school and home with less regard for whether any of this reduces the mother's burden of housework. If he tries something new, he is more likely to be rewarded. The suggestion has also been made that this stress is most productive if it begins at about 6 to 8 years of age.

Dependence and Independence in the Child

The infant and mother establish a close emotional relationship with each other soon after the baby's birth, but the world of the infant soon expands to include others in the family. The classical psychoanalytic view, somewhat difficult to demonstrate clearly but in conformity with much common-sense observation, is that the young child will conclude his infancy period by becoming emotionally attached to the parent of the opposite sex. That is, the boy is more involved emotionally with his mother, while the daughter becomes more attached to her father. The relationship gives pleasure to both partners, but social norms eventually interfere with it. The boy must soon identify with his father, his appropriate role model, if he is to assume an adult male status successfully. It seems likely, as some have asserted, that it is more important for the boy to give up his oedipal tie with his mother, than for the girl to give up her attachment to her father. Assumption of the adult status requires that the male be relatively independent, dominant, and instrumental in social interaction, and to be able to discharge his obligations as head of the family. He cannot, without criticism from others and a feeling of personal failure, move directly from being mother's little boy to being his wife's little boy. By contrast, a girl is permitted to move from being dad's little girl to being her husband's little girl with less criticism. In fact, of course, a large but unknown percentage of people fail to resolve their oedipal ties, and the psychodynamic consequences hamper adult functioning. However, here we are only noting the differences in the *social* patterning of social roles in the two sexes.

Both parents establish love-ties with their children, but use these ties of emotional dependency to force the children gradually toward independence. In a sense, they are partially occupied with forcing the child to develop so that he can leave the family. Other relationships press in the same direction, for adolescent or adult love relationships help the individual in many societies to move out into the world. In a wide range of societies, *peer* groups in the adolescent period also help to set *non-familial* norms, by which the young person adjusts himself and thus can move somewhat away from the family. In the West especially, the combination of peer groups and the impersonal school system weaken the dependence of the young individual on his family. Indeed, it is possible that in any society in which the larger society makes demands or sets norms that are very different from those *within* the family, some types of peer or age groups will arise, to bridge the necessary transition between the two kinds of social structures.

That there is such a gap in Western societies has been asserted time and time again. The phenomenon of "adolescent rebellion" has been viewed with alarm for decades, in perhaps every Western nation. There has been general agreement, although the assertion would be difficult to prove, that parents and youth are in more intense and frequent conflict in modern nations than in other

78

regions or times. We must first keep the problem in perspective by noting that the amount of agreement in modern urban society is far greater than the amount of conflict, even though both parents and adolescents often feel they are locked in an unremitting struggle. Young people actually have much the same opinions on political, theological, and moral questions as their parents, the same tastes in food, clothing, and art—indeed, a reformer must despair, seeing how closely they are aligned on important matters. However, the conflicts do exist, and their roots are interesting, as revealing something of the relations between role patterns in the family and the larger society.[15]

In a period of social change, the society in which the child grows up is different from that in which his parents grew up. The parent calls on *his* childhood experience as a guide, but much of it has become irrelevant, and his standards do not apply any longer. Even if things had not changed, the two sets of people, children and parents, are at different points in their life cycles, and would view differently many kinds of problems and opportunities. Thus, parents and youth are at different points in the long time curve of rapid social change, and at different points in their own life cycles, so that some conflict is inevitable.

An additional tension is inherent in the relations between the two, the fact that parental roles combine authority *and* intimacy. The parent or child may each get his own way through love, but each is called back to socially approved norms by their other needs (e.g., the child needs authority to lean on, to set limits for him) and by the society. As the adolescent moves into adulthood he is constantly threatening the authority of his parents by the simple process of maturation, however he may love them. This recurring tension is intensified in Western societies because there are no well-recognized *steps* by which various areas of authority are gradually relinquished, to make the adjustment easier to tolerate.

In a complex society, and especially in one undergoing rapid change, an adolescent experiences more conflicting norms and competing authorities with each move he makes into the outside world. He can, if he chooses, use them (and every child learns to do this in bargaining with his parents) to justify convenient modes of conduct and of course these modes often violate the wishes of his parents.

In Western countries, the sources of conflict are strengthened further by the fact that the conjugal family is one of intense emotionality, with few kin who can act as buffers or shock-absorbers, and by the fact that Western parents are greatly preoccupied with the sex lives of their children.

[15] This discussion is largely based on Kingsley Davis, "The Sociology of Parent-Youth Conflict," in *American Sociological Review* (1940), 4:523–535.

stratification

eight

Man is an *evaluating* animal. He ranks not only things and activities but also people. One of the results of this evaluative process is the division of societies into classes or levels, such that people in a given class are ranked similarly; but the levels themselves are arranged in a hierarchical order. Which criteria are more or less important for placing people in classes will vary from society to society: courage and skill in war, technical knowledge, literary and humanistic learning, saintliness, or financial success. Stratification systems may also be compared by using several variables, such as the criteria for class placement, how difficult it is to move from class to class, how distinct the classes are, how socially distant the top classes are from the bottom, or how the total population is distributed among the classes.

It is the *family*, not merely the individual, that is ranked in the class structure. The family is the keystone of the stratification system, the social mechanism by which it is maintained. In the interaction of individuals at different class levels, both distance and equality can be observed. The southern plantation owner may talk intimately with one of his tenant farmers, and even share a cup of coffee with him at a local diner, but might not invite him to dinner in a restaurant. He would be still less likely to invite his tenant to a *family* dinner. Marriage, as the linking of two families, is the most complete expression of class equality. Earlier discussions of mate selection pointed out some of the processes that lead to homogamy—the marriage of like with like. It is equally clear that homogamy in turn bolsters the existing class structure.

The interrelationships of family and stratification are many and complex, but may be categorized under two forms: (1) the class distribution of family patterns and processes, how and why family behavior is different in different social strata; and (2) which kinds of family systems are associated with which kinds of stratification systems. For example, are certain patterns of social mobility associated with certain types of family patterns? If position in the stratification system in a given society is based on humanistic learning rather than scientific or technical skill, can we predict what kind of family system will be present? This chapter will focus on the first set of these important interrelationships.

Class Position and Family Variables

Let us begin by briefly examining some of the relations between class position and family variables.

1. In Western countries the age of men at marriage rises with class position.

2. Generally, however, the nobility of Western countries married at younger ages than did other classes.

3. In Western countries, and perhaps generally where there is no frontier land available, farmers marry later than other groups.

4. Toward the upper social strata, young people are granted less freedom of mate choice.

5. When cross-class marriages occur, the woman is more likely than the man to marry upward.

6. In the West the birth rate increases as we approach the lower classes. However, *within* each social ranking or stratum, families with higher income have more children. And very likely in most societies the upper stratum had a higher birth rate, before the introduction of effective contraceptives.

7. Engagement or betrothal is longer toward the upper strata.

8. Where there is a bride price or a dowry system, the economic exchanges between the bride's family and the groom's family are more likely to approach equality toward the upper strata than toward the lower strata.

9. If polygyny is practiced, it is the men of high social or economic position who are more likely to have more than one wife.

10. In the West it is likely that the frequency of sexual intercourse is higher among couples toward the lower strata.

11. When contraceptives are introduced, the upper social strata are more likely to begin using them than are the lower social strata.

12. In the West premarital sexual intercourse begins at an earlier age among men in the lower social strata.

13. In the West extramarital sexual intercourse increases in frequency with increasing age among men in the upper strata, but decreases among men in the lower social strata.

14. The authority of elders and of men is higher toward the upper social strata.

15. The kinship network is more extended toward the upper strata.

16. In the United States upper-class mothers are more likely than middle-class women to justify their demands on children by asserting their authority; middle-class mothers are more likely to appeal to a general moral principle or to a rule originating outside the family circle itself.

17. In the United States middle-class families rear their children more

permissively than do lower-class families, but demand higher achievement in the areas of skill, knowledge, and initiative.

18. The divorce rate is higher toward the lower social strata.

This list is not meant to be complete, and not all these relationships have been definitely proved. Even more important, we cannot explain why or how all the results occur. Such a summary does point out some significant regularities, however, and serves as a point of reference for analyzing the more general processes of interaction between stratification and the family.

Homogamy and Upward Mobility

Let us consider once more the pattern of homogamy. In any stratified society, families, individuals, or castes try to move upward in economic or social ranking, and many succeed. This upward straining is observable, even though people's aspirations may not be high, and their chances of achieving them may be low. However, the very efforts which *individually* are aimed at upward movement, result *collectively* in only modest changes in an individual's social position or the class structure.

This results from two processes. First, part of the individual's class behavior at any level consists in keeping down those who are pushing upward—i.e., trying to keep them from being accepted at the higher level. This may range from refusing to accept a competent Negro as a co-worker or a Jew as a member of a club, to ordering a daughter to stop dating a boy from a poor family. However such behavior may be rationalized, it frustrates in part the efforts of those who wish to achieve equality with those of a higher class level.

Second, if people are striving upward at *every* class level (except the top, where people are trying to hang on) while the competitive advantages of education, family, or friends are set against those who wish to displace the people just above them in class, in general most will stay approximately at the class level where they were born, or move upward only slightly.

Both processes are applicable to the general pattern of homogamy in marriage. Precisely because almost all individuals seek spouses with desirable qualities, those with advantages of wealth, beauty, talent, or prestige *can* obtain spouses like themselves; whereas the less desirable cannot achieve their aspirations, and must marry people much like themselves. Consequently, even in an open-class system most persons marry at about the same class level. Thus, the general shape of the class system may remain relatively stable over generations, not because individuals are content to remain at the same level, or because families *prefer* to find mates for their children who are their equals, but because that is about as much as the individual can command on the marriage market.

We can assume that in societies with more rigid class lines than modern Western societies, there would be fewer cross-class marriages even though no *quantitative* data on a substantial sample seem to be available. In one sample of 2,000 urban households in the city of Bangalore, India, only 9 cross-*caste* unions were discovered. Barber summarizes several sets of related data from prior epochs in the West.[1] For example, the authorities of the city of London in the period after 1360 acted as surrogate parents for orphaned children of merchants, and steered 53 of 63 daughters into marriages with merchants, while the remainder married gentlemen or citizens of lesser guilds. Of 37 widows in the fifteenth century, 22 remarried into the same guild or company as their husbands; two married knights and one a scrivener, while those remaining married into other merchant companies. From the twelfth century on, the

[1] Bernard Barber, *Social Stratification* (New York: Harcourt, Brace & World, 1957), pp. 124 ff.

stratification

French *sergents* (men who administered houses and lands for the nobility) married only within their own class.

Data of this specialized type, though suggestive, give us no exact quantitative estimate of how much homogamy may exist in a given society as a whole. Comparison with the United States is rendered especially difficult by the sifting and bargaining processes of courtship, which we analyzed earlier. The amount of heterogamy may be exaggerated by considering only the class *backgrounds* of the bride and groom and the class position of their families. However, what often appears to be a heterogamous marriage is really a marriage between people whose style of life, tastes, or even incomes are very similar.

Upward mobility of this kind is doubtless typical of other societies as well. In eighteenth-century France, as in China, families moved into the nobility by acquiring wealth and through wealth, position or office. They began to "live nobly"; they built country chateaux and town houses, entertained lavishly and in the latest taste, patronized the arts and letters, and adopted a style of life difficult to differentiate from that of the nobility. Their children were as cultured, talented, and acceptable as those of the nobility—in every way except family history. Money was the marriage link with nobility, but the union was hardly one of fine lord and lowly shepherdess.[2]

The importance of this pattern is evident in a prime consequence of homogamy, the kind of socialization the children of the union will receive. Families that oppose cross-class, cross-ethnic, or cross-religion marriages usually justify their stand by predicting conflict between the spouses, and confusion in the socialization of the child. Equality of background enhances the likelihood that husband and wife will agree on a wide range of matters, and will be better able to rear their children to accept their similar family patterns. Parents generally have to inculcate in their children the values of their own stratum, simply because that is the only class content they themselves understand and accept. This extends to fashions, language, attitudes toward acquiring skills in certain occupations, and tastes in food. In turn, some part of the homogamy pattern derives from the fact that young people simply find one another more or less attractive because of this range of differences or similarities.

The factors that operate to produce marriages predominantly between class equals do not, however, adequately explain the greater control that upper-class families exert over dating, engagement, marriage, and other areas of family interaction. This apparently universal relationship between class and control rests ultimately on the source of stratification itself, the processes of *evaluation*.

As already mentioned, societies differ in their relative emphasis on the different bases of the class system. Courage and skill in war are more important in some, while humanistic knowledge (China) or scientific achievement (the West) may be more important in others. Wealth and the sources of wealth (business, land) may be more or less important. In all societies power can be used to gain prestige, or money can be used to get power; that is, the constituent elements of class position, power, wealth, and prestige, can to some degree be exchanged for one another. But societies vary in the *degree* to which they can be exchanged—e.g., money for a marriage into a noble family, as well as the processes by which the exchange can be carried out.

Whatever assures or yields high class position in a given society, by definition the upper-class families have more of it than do others. In no society do the lower strata in fact have more of the skills, education, mastery of the classics or arts, ability at managing arms and men, or command over the niceties

[2] For an excellent analysis of bourgeois' striving toward nobility, see Elinor G. Barber, *The Bourgeoisie in 18th Century France* (Princeton: Princeton University Press, 1955).

of language and etiquette, than do the upper strata. In addition, in all family systems, upper-class children obtain unearned advantages, entirely irrelevant to their skills or intelligence. Peasant children in fourteenth-century Europe, for example, only rarely had the opportunity to acquire the military skills of the knight, or the intellectual skills of the medieval scholar. Indeed, the rigidity of class barriers is measured by the success of the family system in protecting the inept from open competition, by preventing able lower-class children from obtaining access to the skills and education that permit social mobility.

Differential Family Control

This means, then, that upper-class families in all stratification systems are engaged in a ceaseless struggle to maintain their position, by controlling access to opportunities, preventing acceptance, and by forcing their children to hew to upper-class standards. Since in fact the standards are higher toward the upper strata, the family must expend more energy and resources in dealing with these problems, or eventually lose its position. At the same time, these families have some chance at success, since the amount of resources available for these tasks rises with class position. The upper-class family can hire far more personnel for training its children, far more supervisors to see to it that they do not stray from the prescribed paths.

In addition, upper-class families can control the futures of their children more effectively, since the rebel upper-class child has more to lose than does the rebel lower-class child. In most societies the upper-class family head has been able to invoke both his own power and that of the law to stop a disapproved marriage, and can force some obedience because of his ability to dispense wealth or occupational opportunities. This *differential* control is the key to the resistance of the socially advantaged families to the erosive influence of the industrial system.

Let us consider further the matter of differential family control over its members and especially its children, because it partially resolves an apparent paradox in the relations between industrialization and the family system. As will be discussed in greater detail in the chapter on family change, the spread of industrialism is accompanied by a decline in the extension of kinship networks and the spread of the conjugal system, with its primary emphasis on the nuclear family unit of parents and their children. Various theoretical arguments support the notion that the conjugal family and industrialism "fit"—that the needs of an industrial pattern are better met by the conjugal family system than by any other family system. But, by definition, upper-class families are more in harmony with the industrial economy, since they control it where they do not own it, and can take better advantage of its opportunities and products. Yet their family system is *less* conjugal than the lower-class family system. Its kinship network is larger, it exerts more control over the social lives of children, exercises closer supervision over dating and schools, wields a stronger hand in choice of mate, and so on. Thus the families that seem to be most "out of date" in the modern world are most successful in coping with it.

This paradox can be resolved by glancing at past opportunities in the Western World. Whether we consider the great expansion of ecclesiastical jobs in the eleventh and twelfth centuries, the great increase in political and economic posts in the New World during the sixteenth and seventeenth centuries, or the industrialism of the nineteenth century, families toward the upper strata controlled the more important opportunities because they themselves initiated and were in charge of the new developments. They could obtain obedience

stratification

then, as they can now, because the recalcitrant young family member could be threatened by the loss of both social rank and economic advantage. By contrast, the lower-class family head had no such bargaining power with his sons. If they disobeyed, they lost less. The lower-class family that did not keep its family network active and effective lost less, on the whole, than the upper-class family. After all, the network of the latter contained other higher strata families who themselves would possess benefits and opportunities to exchange.

True enough, the lower-class family member was less encumbered by a large kinship network if he could rise in the social hierarchy, but this was a doubtful blessing, since a young man from a higher class family, though perhaps limited more by kin in his choices of job, location, or wife, could also obtain benefits from them.

The conjugal family system serves well the needs of the modern industrial system—i.e., an open-class system—because the lessened importance of the extended kin permits people to leave their kin easily in order to find a suitable job; and allows the employer generally to ignore kinship ties in seeking the best talent for a job. Nevertheless, within such a system the families of the top strata find it to their advantage to keep their extended kinship ties active, to the extent that these other families also enjoy and can exchange power, privilege, and wealth.

Revolutions are sometimes defined as changes in the stratification system itself—in its *bases*, such as skill in war or ownership of land, and thus in the assumption by a *new class* of the positions of power and prestige. Always this means new *families*, since the revolutionary leaders attempt to legitimize and stabilize their new positions by passing them on to their children. We cannot, therefore, suppose that when families or individuals infiltrate upward from one class to another they are changing the class system. Ordinarily they have no such aim, since thereby they would lose the very advantages they seek by striving upward. The upper bourgeoisie of France in the early eighteenth century had no desire to destroy the aristocratic class (or "estate") system. They simply wanted to move upward in the existing class system.

However, these processes breed some tension. If upper-class families succeed in protecting their inept members and in preventing infiltration from below, armed revolution may occur. Doubtless, most families in all systems attempt this kind of protection, although we do not know as yet which patterns are most successful in achieving that result. In any event, marked success in protecting the individual family may lead to a destruction of the class system itself. On the other hand, talent appears in all strata; if upper-class families permit an easy flow of talent upward, the general structure of the stratification system does not change, but many families will be unable to meet the competition.

Families with advantages are thus always under pressure from other families that want those advantages. No system has yet been devised which could protect upper-class families from the vicissitudes of mortality, failure of talent and energy, inability to socialize their children effectively, or low fertility. Though upper-class families may protect *individuals* from rigorous competition, these families as *groups* or networks cannot avoid competition themselves, including pressures from those striving upward. Indeed, families that zealously protect their members from competition may ruin themselves by failing to socialize their offspring effectively enough to assume family leadership in the next generation.

Hsu argues that this was a major factor in the class mobility of the Chinese system. Often the family head permitted his sons to become wastrels, enjoying their irresponsibility and loose or luxurious way of living as a sign of his own worldly success. Since they were not held to performance standards as youngsters, however, they were unable as adults to hold the family or its property intact.[3]

Class Stability

The effect of these competitive processes is clear: The apparent stability of great families is an illusion; few retain their positions over many generations. As mentioned earlier, various studies of mobility under several Chinese dynasties show that over one third of the elite in any generation were from non-elite families.[4] An inquiry into the 1547 noble Swedish families that were listed in 1626 showed that 84 per cent had been wiped out by the third generation, or were surviving because of the marriage of a daughter. Only 2 families out of this large group survived for 9 generations. The upper class in the United States has been similarly unstable. Research into the continuity of English nobility from the mid-1600's to the mid-1900's also discloses a high rate of turnover.[5]

It should be kept in mind that upper-strata families are vying not only with upwardly moving lower-strata families, but also with *one another*. A family whose fertility is low may die out, but families with excessive fertility may be unable to provide for all their members and have to watch some of their kin sink to lesser positions in the society. Economic or governmental expansion, war and colonial growth, may take care of some of them. On the other hand, until the Napoleonic Wars it was the nobility who bore arms, so that war often depleted their ranks. War, then, not only reduced the number of surviving noble sons but also offered opportunities to lower-strata sons, who rose from their poor beginnings through military distinction.

Although upper-strata elders in all societies have more power than elders in other strata, it seems likely that where the stratification system is based on individual achievement (as in industrial societies) a *high* degree of control by elders is difficult to maintain, except under special structural arrangements. One such set of patterns was to be found in classical China. There the young individual himself never alone possessed the wealth and leisure that were necessary to permit the many years of full-time dedication to learning the classics, law, philosophy, and calligraphy that were the subjects of the civil-service examinations. He needed both talent and a large investment to prepare for the successive tests which were hurdles in the path of a successful mandarin. Thereby, he incurred heavy obligations to his family or clan as well as to his ancestors. Perhaps equally significant, achievement meant not merely learning but also living a well-rounded life that expressed an inner harmony. The individual who repudiated either his ancestors or his elders would have hindered his own ascent. His behavior would have been regarded as a grave defect in his own spiritual fitness for higher posts.

Stratification and Family Roles

The U.S. achievement system shares with the other industrial nations of the West the peculiarity of emphasizing performance in a *job*. Social position in most societies has stressed, far more than in our system,

[3] Francis L. K. Hsu, *Under the Ancestors' Shadows* (New York: Columbia University Press, 1948), especially Chap. 10.
[4] Robert M. Marsh, in *The Mandarins* (Glencoe, Ill.: The Free Press, 1961), presents his own research and summarizes prior work on mobility.
[5] Bernard Barber, *Social Stratification*, pp. 423–427; see also the discussion of mobility in France in the work by Elinor G. Barber, already cited.

stratification

performance in a range of several kinds of tasks, but not primarily in a specific job. For example, the Roman elite were expected to become military commanders. Their social position, however, did not rest on this achievement, but rather on inherited status and on their ownership and management of land. A job-based system, of course, reduces the general authority of family elders.

Our stratification system differs also in its nearly complete lack of sumptuary legislation and a relative lack of external symbols of status—anyone may wear any kind of clothing he can purchase. The openness of class is expressed by this lack of a sharp discrimination or segregation of classes from one another. General distinctions are visible, but primarily between wide points on the social scale, and even these are sometimes confused by "bad" taste or "good" taste at unexpected points.

Another point at which the relatively lesser control by elders is seen is the pattern of neolocality, by which young couples move away from the older generation geographically, and thus can avoid more easily their attempts to guide their lives. The free choice of mate is another index of lesser control.

These several factors combine at one interesting juncture, the crucial class importance of courtship for the *female*. Her future rank is mainly determined by the *future job* achievement of the man she marries, rather than by the class position of his family. Even if she has wealth, he is supposed to perform well in a job; failure causes some loss of esteem even though their standard of living is not affected. Presumably, this set of factors is one source of the great amount of attention given to feminine glamour in our society. The woman is in a marketing situation in which she must do her own advertising.

In such a society the elders have a rather ambiguous status. Because of intensive job specialization, there is statistically less likelihood that any given man in an advantageous position can help any kinsman obtain the specific job he wants to get. Kinship influence can be important, but it is usually confined to a narrow range of job possibilities. Where the stratification system is based on land, as in peasant societies, the old can gradually retire, maintaining some real and much symbolic authority (as owner or trustee of the land) over his family until death. In addition, the old are more likely to have acquired substantial knowledge about the management of land and men, not to be easily acquired by reading books.

By contrast, in our own society when a man leaves his job he becomes completely removed from it, losing the major source of his social position without compensatory status benefits. Only rarely can he pass on his job to his son. For technical knowledge, our society also relies on professionals or the books they write, rather than on the accumulated knowledge of elders. Thus in a conflict of wills with his son, the elder has less bargaining power. The society gives no *special* role to land-ownership, for it has come to mean only equivalent wealth. Even the upper-class family is not likely to maintain the same estate for generations. Thus the continuity of the family is not identified with continuity of land-ownership.

One interesting consequence of these intertwined factors has been a change in the attitudes of older people with respect to their responsibility for the next generation. Few men now try to build fortunes, or even a substantial inheritance, for their children. The older generation instead accepts the responsibility for giving the younger an education—i.e., the skill-capital for holding a *job*. One facet of this change is that parents increasingly assert their right to have some fun with their money, too. Social-security provisions may have been expanding over the past few decades, as some assert, because the young can no longer be counted on to take care of the old adequately. The other side of this

87

coin is equally worth investigating. The old feel less responsibility for their adult sons and daughters as well.

Class Position and Divorce

The relation between class position and divorce is complex, and conditioned by many historical factors. An accumulation of research data had demonstrated by the early 1950's that there is an *inverse* correlation between class ranking and the divorce rate in the United States. However, it seems equally clear that this was *not* the usual relationship in the past. Yet it may be possible that the present inverse relation between class position and divorce rate well expresses the generally greater marital instability in lower social strata. In order to unravel these patterns, we shall have to consider both historical facts and cross-national data.

Owing to the close relationship in Western countries between the position of the Church and the civil laws on divorce, it was either impossible or extremely difficult in all Western countries to dissolve marraiges by divorce until the twentieth century. Even at present, Ireland, Portugal, Spain, and Italy do not permit divorce, although Protestants in Portugal and Spain may obtain divorces. The older legal Church separation "from bed and board" is possible in both Catholic and Protestant countries—i.e., a separation without the right to remarry. Moreover, until late in the nineteenth century, the administration of divorce law was in the hands of the elite, who had little interest in the marital problems of the poor. Consequently, the *only* people who could obtain a divorce at all were upper-class individuals. In many states in this country it was possible to obtain a divorce only by special act of the state legislature. In England until 1857, only by act of Parliament could a couple obtain a divorce. Thus, whatever the rate of marital *instability* (desertion, disharmony, separation), the rate of divorce in the U.S. was higher in the upper classes until some period in the late nineteenth century or the early twentieth century. We shall look at the pattern in other countries subsequently.

One such factor is the greater material difficulty of life in the lower social strata, and thus the possibility that couples will *displace* their irritation from economic sources onto other areas of marital life. This is especially likely in the United States, where the lack of rigid class definitions means that people cannot be easily content with their lot. A second factor is that a higher proportion of women obtain sexual satisfaction in marriage toward the upper social strata, a higher proportion of men enjoy their work, and a higher proportion of couples make high marital adjustment scores, so that they have less wish to escape from the marriage.

Next, a higher proportion of income is committed toward the upper strata; that is, it is expended on insurance, houses, private education, and so on, and thus cannot be easily shifted as an adjustment to the economic problems of divorce. Withdrawing support creates more problems at the upper-income levels than the the lower, and arouses more social censure. This is accentuated by the greater differential between a wife's potential earnings and her husband's at the higher social level, as against those at a lower level. The woman is somewhat more dependent on her husband and has less reason to leave him, but correlatively she also receives more legal protection.

It is probable that divorce attitudes are somewhat more liberal among the upper-social strata. However, the social and kinship networks are more extensive and more stable, so that a marital disruption is more likely to create problems in personal or kinship relations. The middle- or upper-class person cannot evade his marital obligations by leaving his spouse, since anonymity is not possible.

88

Table 1

**Proneness to Divorce by Urban Occupation,
United States, April, 1949 ***

Occupation	Index of Proneness to Divorce
Professional	67.7
Proprietors, managers, officials	68.6
Clerical, sales	71.8
Craftsmen, foremen	86.6
Operators (semiskilled)	94.5
Service workers	254.7
Laborers (except farm and mine)	180.3

* This and the following two tables are from William J. Goode, "Family Disorganization," in Robert K. Merton and Robert A. Nisbet (eds.), *Contemporary Social Problems* (New York: Harcourt, Brace & World, 1961), pp. 417–418, 422.

Table 2

**Proneness to Divorce Index, by Income,
Population Aged 25–44 Years, 1950**

Income (1949)	Index
$0	199.0
1–999	188.6
1,000–1,999	134.8
2,000–2,999	92.9
3,000–3,999	89.2
4,000 and over	66.7

Table 3

**Ratios of Per Cent of Non-White Divorced
to Per Cent of White Divorced (1890–1950)**

	1890	1900	1910	1920	1930	1940	1950
Ratios:	1.24	1.95	1.67	1.52	1.50	0.95	1.04

Desertion is getting more and more difficult with our growing system of bureaucratic records and remains a genuine possibility only for the lower-class person.

These factors are at work in creating a higher divorce rate among the lower strata, whether we use occupation, income, or education to index class position. If we relate the percentage divorced in a given segment of the population to the percentage which that segment furnishes of the total population, we can see whether each segment produces a high or low number of divorces. Thus, if factory workers constitute 25 per cent of the adult population, but 35 per cent of the divorced population, their index of proneness to divorce would be 140; if they constituted 25 per cent of the divorced population, of course, their index would be 100—i.e., they constitute the same proportion of the divorced as they do of the labor force. Here, we shall have to use data from 1949, since those from the 1960 census are not yet available. We may add to this the fact that divorce rate among non-Whites has been greater than for Whites for many decades, with the exception of the intercensal decade 1930–1940.

89

From these data, it is clear that the divorce rate decreases as we near the upper social strata, but that the differences vary when we use one index of class rather than another. For education, the differences are slight even if we ignore the "no schooling" group as being primarily rural people in isolated areas where resort to divorce court is not common, and the "not known" group as being men living in depressed urban areas, with little education. However, those with more education seem to divorce less than those with less education. On the other hand, among non-Whites, a strong positive correlation between education and divorce existed in 1950. Notice also that the ratios between non-White and White divorce proneness seems to decline gradually over the decades, suggesting a closer approximation between White and Negro patterns.

This historical pattern, a movement from a higher divorce rate among the *upper* social strata, to a lower divorce rate, could be expected to occur in all Western countries as they become industrialized and change their court systems to permit the lower social strata easy and cheap access to the divorce courts. Presumably, farming populations would have lower divorce rates, but within the agricultural groups the upper strata should have lower rates than the lower strata. The inverse class differential in divorce rates already exists in New Zealand, Australia, Sweden, Belgium, and France. In England and Wales, the *trend* in this direction is clear from 1871–1951.[6] In Yugoslavia a somewhat higher divorce rate still exists among the upper occupational groups.

If the forces making for marital breakup are stronger toward the lower social strata, then in societies in which there is a relatively "free divorce market" (i.e., where divorce procedures have not been in the hands of the elite, but rather in the hands of the family itself) we should expect to find higher divorce rates, or a higher percentage of divorced, toward the lower social strata. Data for Arab countries are not clear, in part because of registration and tabulation difficulties. Over the past generation, the new Arab leaders have come to disapprove of the older system of relatively free divorce. Quantitative data are not available for India. However, divorce was almost impossible for Brahmins, the upper caste, until recently (1955), although it was not difficult for lower castes and outcastes. In this case, however, religious prescriptions may be more important than class differential marital strains.

For Japan, quantitative data show a definite rise in divorce with level of occupation. Contemporary quantitative data to test this notion for China are not available, but under the older family patterns divorce was much less possible for members of the upper classes than for those of the lower classes.

[6] These data are presented in my "Marital Satisfaction and Instability. A Cross-Cultural Class Analysis of Divorce Rates," in *International Social Science Journal* (1962), 507–526.

dissolution
of family
role systems

nine

Family disorganization is a common topic of gossip, partly because everyone may suffer one or another of its various types, and because these experiences are likely to be dramatic, embodying difficult moral choices and personal adjustments. All of us die, to leave a gap in the role system of our family. Many of us divorce or are children of divorce. And many who are not touched by divorce know that their seemingly unbroken family is no more than a façade, hiding people who do not truly share the same home.

Family disorganization may be defined as "the breakup of a family unit, the dissolution or fracture of a structure of social roles when one or more members fail to perform adequately their role obligations." [1] Under this definition the main types of family disorganization are the following:

1. *Illegitimacy.* This is the *uncompleted* family unit. It may be included here, along with other forms of role failures in the family, because the "father-husband" is missing and therefore does not perform his duties as these are defined by the society or by the mother. In addition, at least one source of il-

---

[1] William J. Goode, "Family Disorganization," in Robert K. Merton and Robert A. Nisbet (eds.), *Contemporary Social Problems* (New York: Harcourt, Brace & World, 1961), p. 370.

legitimacy is to be found in the failure of family members of both the mother and father to carry out their role obligations.

2. *Annulment, separation, divorce, and desertion.* Here family dissolution occurs because one spouse or both decide to leave each other, and thus cease to discharge their role obligations.

3. *"Empty shell family."* Here family members continue to dwell together but have little communication or interaction with one another and especially fail to give emotional support to one another.

4. *Unwilled absence of one spouse.* Some families dissolve because the husband or wife has died, or is jailed, or is separated from the family because of wars, depression, or some other catastrophe.

5. *"Unwilled" major role failures.* Catastrophes within the family may include severe mental, emotional, or physical pathologies. A child may be mentally retarded, or a child or spouse may become psychotic. Serious and continuing medical pathologies may also cause a major role failure.

In the following discussion we shall emphasize divorce and death more than other catastrophes, but a more complete discussion would include all of them. Illegitimacy has already been treated earlier in this volume, but with only slight emphasis on the role failures involved in the phenomenon.

A glance at this range of processes and events suggests that everyone eventually witnesses or experiences some form of family disorganization. Notice, too, that the larger society is more concerned with certain forms of disorganization than with others and attempts to impose solutions for them. The society is likely to be concerned about a case of illegitimacy, for example, and recently social agencies have become somewhat concerned with the impact of severe mental retardation or emotional or mental sickness on the role structure of the family, and have begun to offer professional help in an attempt to solve this problem. The formal agencies of the society are virtually unconcerned with the "empty shell family," however, and no official procedures exist by which outside agencies can intervene in such cases.

The rate of family disorganization of all types remains unknown. Except for divorce and death, we do not know how many families in any nation suffer or have suffered from one or more of these difficulties. Even when a society exhibits a high rate of disorganization of one type, this does not mean that the family system is breaking up, or even changing. For example, the divorce rate in Japan during the early Meiji period (after 1868) was extremely high, as it was in Arab countries during the same period. However, both these great cultures had had high divorce rates prior to the modern period.

Major changes in family systems, because they introduce new values, usually mean an increase in role failure. Since some people will accept the new ways and others will not, there is considerable disagreement over what the role obligations really are. Necessarily, then, many people will be judged to have failed in their role obligations, by either the new or the old standards.

Divorce may be seen as a personal misfortune for one or both spouses in any society, but it must also be viewed as a social invention, one type of escape valve for the inevitable tensions of marriage itself. Not only is divorce permitted in nearly all the world's societies, but in most primitive societies the rate of divorce has been higher than in the contemporary United States.[2] In addition, a few nations have had higher divorce rates than the United States

---

[2] George P. Murdock, "Family Stability in Non-European Cultures," *Annals of the American Academy of Political and Social Science* (November 1950), 272:167.

dissolution of family role systems

at different times in the past, for example Japan in the period 1887–1919; Algeria, 1887–1940; Israel, 1935–1944; and Egypt, 1935–1954.

But though divorce is common among the world's societies, it does express a high degree of hostility between husband and wife and breaks the bonds which once united two family lines. It inevitably creates serious adjustment problems for the adults and children concerned. Consequently, even in societies with a relatively high divorce rate there is no substantial approval of divorce. Rather, various procedures or mechanisms are evolved by which divorce is kept at a lower rate than would occur without these patterns. The degree to which these mechanisms are successful will determine in part whether the divorce rate is high or low.

One universal pattern, noted earlier, is the attempt on the part of families to marry their youngsters to spouses of about the same social background. This means that both will have similar habits and tastes, thus eliminating many areas of potential disagreement.

Secondly, all societies define certain kinds of disagreements and difficulties as unimportant, and not to be used as a basis for divorce. Of course, what is trivial and what is important will vary from one society to another. For example, in classical China any disrespect on the part of the woman toward her husband's elder relatives was regarded as adequate grounds for divorce. On the other hand, though Western countries require young spouses to be civil to their parents-in-law, neither is required to be especially deferential toward them. Some annoyances are socially defined as characteristic of the sex and thus not to be taken seriously. For example, U.S. husbands typically complain that their wives cannot handle the budget, that they are not on time, and care too much about clothing; but these traits are viewed as "typical of women" and not grave enough to justify a divorce.

Another pattern by which marital tension and unhappiness are kept within some bounds is simply to lower the *expectations* about what marital life will bring. In Western societies the young person is given a rather romantic view of marriage and love, and is disappointed to find that marriage is at best contented and dull, and at worse a perceptual ache. In most societies, however, the young were taught that at best they could count on respect and a proper discharge of duties from their spouse, but they could not expect happiness and naturally could not divorce if they failed to achieve happiness.

An additional mode of avoiding marital tension has been prevalent in pre-industrial societies, and was mentioned earlier: The focus of family life is not on the marital relation of husband and wife, but rather on a larger extended family, the lineage, or the clan. Consequently, even if the two spouses do not get along well together, that is not judged to be important as long as their behavior toward their more extended kin is rated as proper, and they carry out their parental tasks adequately.

As is clear, societies vary in the use they make of such techniques for keeping marital tension lower than it would otherwise be. Societies also vary in their definitions of (1) how much any person should bear or tolerate before seeking a formal solution to his marital problem; and (2) what are the permissible solutions. Husbands and wives in this country in the nineteenth century were willing to tolerate a far higher level of discord before seeking a divorce than their counterparts are today.

As to the solutions for marital hostility, in some Western countries (Spain, Ireland, Italy, and Brazil) only legal separations are permitted, and thus husbands and wives may not seek new spouses. In both Italy and Brazil,

Table 4

Divorce Rates, 1910–1956,
Selected Western Countries

Country	Number of Divorces Per 1,000 Marriages	
	1910	1956
United States	87.4	246.2
Germany	30.2	89.2
England and Wales	2.2 (1911)	74.4
Australia	12.9	90.4
France	46.3	100.5
Sweden	18.4	175.4 *

* Data from official sources. A ratio between the number of divorces in a given year and the number of marriages in a given year does not, of course, state the changes of *eventual* divorce. Obviously, the divorces in a given year do not primarily come from the marriages in the same year. On the other hand, a more correct figure, the number of divorces for each year per 1,000 existing marriages, is obtainable in only a few countries. When the divorce rate is *rising*, divorces in any given year come from marriages in the prior decade for the most part and thus the ratio of divorces to marriages in a given year underestimates the likelihood of those marriages ending in divorce.

separations are rather common. In a 1955 speech proposing certain divorce grounds, an Italian deputy asserted that some 40,000 couples separate legally or informally. In such societies men are usually allowed to enter a new union by taking a mistress, but women are rather more restricted. Under the older Chinese family system, a man might introduce a concubine into his own household as one solution for his marital difficulty.

Rise in the Divorce Rate

In spite of the personal unhappiness caused by divorce, and the widespread condemnation of its spread, divorce rates have been rising in all Western countries. In most, the rates have been rising faster than in the United States, where the increase began a century ago. This change is the result of the interaction of several factors. Perhaps the most important is the lessened *disapproval* of divorce itself. It is safe to say that half a century ago, almost anyone who divorced lost some esteem in his social circle, if he was not cast out entirely. Second, the *alternatives* available to the divorcée have also changed. Since many other people have divorced, it is likely that a new mate will become available in time. Between 85 per cent and 90 per cent of those who divorce between the ages of 20–40 are likely to remarry. Moreover, since few people now live on farms, the services formerly provided by the spouse can be bought from specialists. It is possible for a divorced woman to support herself, even though her own salary will not be as large as that of a man. Correspondingly, the social *pressures* from friends and kin to stay married are weaker than they were half a century ago.

In Table 4 the rise in divorce rate for selected Western countries is shown.

Proneness to Divorce

Which couples are more likely to divorce? If the decision to divorce is a function of the predisposition of the spouses relating to

94

dissolution of family role systems

divorce, the alternatives both negative and positive to their present relationship, and the pressures and counter-pressures from friends and kin, then we should expect that people in different social positions are more or less likely to experience a divorce in their lifetime. They may have received a somwhat different socialization, belong to different religious sects, have different expectations regarding the appropriate way of conducting a marriage, and see a greater or lesser moral error in entering a new marriage, and thus are more or less prone to divorce.

For example, we mentioned earlier that the divorce rate is high in matrilineal societies, that marital adjustment is low among couples with very dissimilar backgrounds, and that the divorce rate is higher toward the lower social strata. Let us look at other differences in proneness to divorce.

Among the farming population of the Western countries, the divorce rate is higher for landowners than for farm laborers. Rural people in these countries have somewhat more conservative attitudes toward divorce, and thus generally lower rates of divorce, than do urban dwellers. In the United States this difference has not been significant. However, in Japan and the Arab countries, the divorce rate has generally been higher in rural populations, in part because they were mainly lower-class persons for whom divorce was not so great a tragedy nor so unfamiliar an event. Thus the gradual introduction of the modern conjugal family system, fragile as its units are, may actually decrease the rate of divorce among agriculturalists in this segment of the world's population.

Although U.S. churches do not approve of divorce, they vary in the degree to which they deplore or condemn it. Consequently, divorce differentials by church affiliation should exist. However, it is difficult to measure to what degree the members of different churches are prone to divorce, since the U.S. Census has never asked for the religious affiliation of the population, and thus the basic data are lacking. On the other hand, a number of surveys have been taken here and there by sociologists and by churches themselves.

As a consequence, we can present a few findings about the relation between divorce and religious affiliation. It must be emphasized, of course, that these studies do not typically ascertain how devout a believer in the doctrines of his church the respondent is, but merely relate marital status or divorce experience to formal church affiliation. The findings may be summarized as follows:

Jews have about as high a divorce rate as that of the general population. However, two studies report that when both spouses are Jewish, the proneness to divorce is about as low as when both are Catholic.

In two-thirds of the new desertion cases in Philadelphia, one or both parties were Catholic, thus suggesting an over-representation of Catholics.

Generally a marriage between two spouses belonging to the same church is less prone to divorce. When both are of the same religion, few or no differences appear between the rates of Jews, Protestants, or Catholics, according to three available studies. Other evidence indicates that marriages between two Catholics are about one-half to two-thirds as likely to end in divorce as are Protestant marriages.

People without religious affiliations have the highest divorce rate, and the next highest is found among marriages of mixed faiths.

Among marriages of mixed faiths, some analysts have suggested that the rate is highest when the Catholic husband is married to a Protestant wife. As already noted earlier, marriages between Catholics and Protestants seem to be

95

becoming more common, amounting to between 5 per cent and 50 per cent of marriages involving Catholics in different regions of the United States.[3]

The sociological factors that might create these apparent differences should be evident. First, churches vary in their opposition to divorce, but church membership alone does not determine whether or not couples will divorce. As already mentioned, many other variables other than predisposition toward or against divorce must be considered. In addition, the total voluntary marital dissolution rate—that is, including *all* forms of voluntary abdication of role obligations, not merely divorce—may be almost as high among people who are violently opposed to divorce as among the rest of the population. Second, those who are affiliated with no church are likely to be less ideologically opposed to divorce, and moreover may be deviant in other minor ways, and thus their divorce rate is somewhat higher.

Third, any form of interfaith marriage is an index of the different social backgrounds of the husband and wife, and thus might be expected to lead to a somewhat higher divorce rate. On the other hand, those who are willing to move outside their own church to find a spouse are also likely to be less strong in their faith, and so the lower intensity of belief would mean less conflict over religious matters. In any event, it seems likely that the differences in behavior between those who are non-believers and those who are faithful adherents of a church are likely to be greater than the differences among those who belong to different churches.

Finally, it seems likely that there will be more conflict in interfaith marriages, between a Catholic husband and a Protestant wife. In interfaith marriages the Catholic father is more likely to insist that his children be reared as Catholics than the Protestant father is to insist that his children be reared as Protestants. In addition, when the wife is Catholic and the husband is Protestant, she is likely to tolerate more conflict than the Protestant woman would before initiating a divorce suit. (In most instances it is the woman who initiates the suit.)

To these associations between social backgrounds and divorce a few additional ones should be added. One is the greater proneness to divorce when marriage occurs at very young ages (15 to 19 years). Another is the disapproval of the marriage by kin or friends, and differing opinions of husband and wife with reference to their mutual role obligations. The importance of both factors would seem to be generally self-evident, but a brief comment should be made with reference to the disapproval by kin or friends of the marriage. This may be seen as an index of two sets of factors. One is the simple prediction that kin and friends make about the possible success of the marriage. After all, they do know one or both spouses-to-be. In addition, however, their support may also be a direct factor in binding the couple together.

Analysis of why people divorce, like the analysis of any major decision that takes place over a long period of time, is especially difficult. As already noted, it is compounded of the values and predispositions of the couples, the relative weights of satisfactions and dissatisfactions as against the realistic alternatives they face, the social pressures from kin and friends, and, of course, many precipitating factors. Couples who divorce are willing to list their complaints, but a list of these complaints merely informs us how many *areas of life*

---

[3] These items and the accompanying citations are from Goode, "Family Disorganization," in Merton and Nisbet (eds.), *Contemporary Social Problems*, p. 424. The third study suggesting that the Catholic-Catholic divorce rate is not much lower than that of other religiously homogamous marriages is a recent unpublished work by Ernest W. Burgess and Peter C. Pineo.

dissolution of family role systems

marriage touches: They are dissatisfied in almost every area in which they come into contact with each other.

Such complaints must be separated from the *grounds* for divorce. These vary from state to state and from nation to nation, but they merely tell us something about the legal system under which divorces are granted. In general, people use as grounds for their divorce suit whatever legal charges will enable them to obtain a divorce relatively easily, with as little stigma or scandal as possible. In the United States about three-fifths of all divorces are granted on grounds of "cruelty," which has come to mean almost any kind of behavior that the judge will accept as sufficient cause for terminating the marriage.

Neither a listing of all the complaints made by divorced spouses nor a listing of the grounds for divorce will give us sufficient data for understanding the divorce process. Perhaps we shall not comprehend it fully without *longitudinal* studies of large samples of couples, following them through the vicissitudes of marriage and divorce or death over their lifetimes.

Sexual Adjustment and Divorce

Without attempting such a task now, we may consider a few of the complexities of just one factor in divorce and marital happiness, the sexual adjustment of the couple.

Modern analysts of divorce have agreed that a change in the importance of sex relations in marriage has occurred over the past generation. After World War I the sexual expectations of women became somewhat higher. Over the past several decades, husbands doubtless have improved their sex techniques in an effort to please their wives more fully, and wives have become less frigid, less difficult to please. On the other hand, many couples who divorce do complain of sexual problems. The marriage analyst's interpretation is that these are not primary, and that they are rather created by the underlying conflicts and tension of marriage. Consequently, unsatisfactory sexual relations as a *cause* of divorce would seem to be of relatively minor importance.

One difference in sex roles should be noted here: Men are more likely than women to complain of problems in sexual relations, but primarily because these are more important to men's general evaluation of a marriage than they are to the wives' satisfaction with *their* entire marriage relationship.

Sex Roles and Divorce

Data from several surveys suggest that women complain more about their marriages than do men. The reason seems to lie in the greater significance of the marriage for women, their greater dependence on its success and satisfaction for their general adjustment to living itself. Correspondingly, about three-fourths of all divorces in the United States are granted to women.

Nevertheless, one study develops the theory that *husbands* first want to break up the marriage more often than do wives. Much of the husband's energy, attention, and concern are focused on things outside the home. He may engage in behavior which would not be considered legitimate or innocent if his wife were to engage in it. He may, without criticism, have far more cross-sex friendships. As a consequence, he is less committed to the home than is the wife, and is more likely to find fun, diversion, and even involvement away from home.

On the other hand, under modern egalitarian norms, this behavior is likely to make the wife unhappy. However, precisely because the man's outside life is so important to him, his wife has less bargaining power in forcing him to conform to her wishes. The wife is less likely at first to want a divorce, while a husband is more likely to feel guilty about demanding it. The outcome seems to be that the man is likely to develop a pattern of behavior which elicits criticism, condemnation, and disrespect from her as part of a spiral of increasing conflict between the two. That is, by making himself objectionable, he arouses in his wife (with or without *planning* to do so) a wish to break the marriage also. The criticism which he undergoes in the process is likely also to assuage some of the feelings of guilt he might otherwise suffer.

Adjustment to Death and Divorce

Perhaps everyone dies a little when, as in divorce, a tie that began in love ends in hostility, with neither person totally innocent and neither really intending such an outcome. Because of this destructive element in divorce, many social analysts have pointed to the similarities between the adjustment to divorce and to death. This is a way of asserting that the real meaning of death is social, not biological. The unique qualities of each relationship make the universal experience of death peculiarly painful: No one can truly replace the person who has died.

But though each death and each divorce is unique, those who suffer them share many common experiences. They begin with certain similarities in the life situation of both the bereaved and the divorced. These may be briefly listed:

1. The cessation of sexual satisfaction.
2. The loss of friendship, love, or security.
3. The loss of an adult role model for children to follow.
4. The increase in the domestic workload for the remaining spouse, especially in the handling of children.
5. The increase in economic problems, especially if the husband has died or left the home.
6. A redistribution of household tasks and responsibilities.

However, as against these similarities a *fundamental* difference between the two problems of adjustment should be kept in mind. In *all* societies the rituals and customs of death and bereavement are woven closely into the web of the institutional fabric. Role obligations and rights are rather closely specified, and supported by kin and friends.

However, in some societies—Western countries are the most conspicuous example—the patterns of post-divorce adjustment are not well institutionalized.

Let us first consider a case, that of the Arabs, in which a high divorce rate has been part of the family tradition for many generations.

Under Arab custom some part of the bride price (from one-third to one-half) was not paid at the time of the marriage, but had to be paid if there was a divorce. This served as a small deterrent to a man's whimsical decision to cast his wife aside. Among the wealthy, marriage exchanges were costly and first wives at least were also likely to be from high-ranking families. Since, in addition, a man might add a wife or concubine if his first wife displeased him, he had little motivation to divorce.

At all levels of rank and wealth there was a fairly strong feeling that a man should not divorce a woman who had borne him sons. Thus divorce was more likely to occur among social strata that had invested little money in the specific marriage (so that there would be little litigation over the division of property), and among couples with few children.

Under Mohammedan law, a woman was heiress to part of her family property, entitled to one-half a brother's share. She did not take this property, but as a consequence always had some moral right to being cared for by her father's line. Thus, when she returned to her paternal family after she divorced, she could count on support.

98

If her children were very young, she would take them with her, but there was no doubt about who was responsible for their care—her former husband. In addition, her own family could count on receiving an additional bride price from a second marriage, for the high rate of marital turnover almost guaranteed that a second husband would be available.

Finally, the marriage was not likely to have been based on a love relationship to begin with, so that the emotional trauma of divorce would not be great. These arrangements meant, then, that most of the loose ends created by divorce were dealt with.

Similarly, in most primitive societies the place of the child was always clear. If it was a matrilineal society, the child belonged with its mother's line; if patrilineal, with the father's line. In a matrilineal system the man could return to his mother's home and expect to be welcomed there. A divorce required the return of a bride price, but in a society where the divorce rate is high, the bride price is low, so that no great difficulties ensue. Here again, then, the specific obligations and statuses of all persons concerned are known in advance, so that post-divorce problems are minimized.

In Western countries, by contrast, few structural arrangements exist for handling the problems of post-divorce adjustment. The divorcée is neither single nor married. His or her family and friends have no real obligation to help arrange a new marriage. It is unclear what the former husband's and wife's obligations to each other are. Only legal rulings define the obligations of the father to his children. He is rarely granted custody, and over time may see his children so seldom as to lose his willingness to obey even the legal stipulations.

On the other hand, both friends and kin feel a strong moral obligation to help a widower or widow, and to comfort him or her. The bereaved person is allowed to grieve publicly, but in a social situation of considerable control. Moreover, by being forced to move through a set of rituals, the bereaved person is reminded of the obligation to remain part of the social group. Both friends and kin attempt to interpret the meaning of death, and in this expression of concern some solace is obtained.

Kin are also morally required to help if called on, and they do not face a situation of divided loyalties as they typically do when the family is disorganized by divorce. Dead spouses are good spouses. If there was hostility between family and in-laws, or family feuds, these are to a large extent set aside. Most spouses who survive feel some guilt about it, but the customs and rituals of death give the surviving person considerable support. By contrast, the guilt arising from divorce is not assuaged by institutionally required reassurances. No one is obligated to rally around.

One is supposed to sympathize with the surviving family members; it is not clear in the case of divorce, however, whether one should give sympathy or instead offer a toast and begin to help the divorcée find a new partner.

In nearly all societies, the woman is more likely to be a widow than the husband is likely to be a widower, because the male mortality rate is higher. Moreover, the death of a husband sets off a more elaborate series of death rituals, because he is regarded as socially of more consequence. His loss is viewed as having more impact on the family structure.

The mourning which is psychodynamically necessary to integrate fully the death of a spouse into the life pattern of the surviving spouse is guided in more detail in non-Western countries. A widow is usually required to exhibit her status as widow longer than the man must officially mourn for his wife. In India the Brahmin widow was not supposed to remarry at all, and apparently there was considerable conformity to this rule until recently, so much so that the fertility rate of Brahmins has been lower than that of the other major Indian castes.

In China, and to a lesser extent in Japan, the same rule held. Demographic evidence suggests that widows did in fact marry, though doubtless this occurred far more frequently in the lower social strata than in the upper.

The idealization of what the wife owed to her former husband is probably tied to the definition of the woman as dependent on the man. The injunction to remain faithful to him even after death doubtless intensified the rule by which she was to remain faithful to him while he was alive.

Because the social meaning of age differs in men and women, so that an older man may marry a younger woman, and because societies almost never enjoin celibacy on the widower, the widower is much more likely to find a new spouse than is the widow. In the United States about twice as many widowers as widows remarry during the first 5 years after their spouses die.

On the other hand, the Western countries have generally dropped their detailed rules about the length of mourning periods, including the disapproval of those who remarry soon after their spouse dies. There are now few or no formal rules governing the length of the mourning period, and men and women who remarry relatively early are not criticized severely. Moreover, the changing definitions of age and the insistence of both the younger and older generations that the older people should live in separate households both press toward remarriage as a form of adjustment. Finally, since an increasing number of divorcées are available for remarriage, the chances of remarriage for both widows and widowers are much higher than they were a generation ago.

In Western countries no moral norm states that people should remarry after divorce or bereavement, but innumerable social pressures lead toward that solution. Adults in our society live in couples, entertain in couples, and converse with one another about their family units. The formerly married person who is not now married does not fit these arrangements easily. Taking care of children without a spouse is wearying and difficult. The children themselves, accustomed to pair relationships, are likely to suggest to their parents, whether divorced, widowed, or widowered, that they remarry. Friends are likely to introduce them to eligible partners. In spite of the somewhat greater tolerance in our generation of sexual relations outside marriage, these are likely to be awkward, tedious, or embarrassing if they are continued for a long period of time without legitimation by marriage.

It seems likely that most people began to take part in a courtship and dating process before they have fully adjusted to the loss of their former spouse, whether by divorce or death. Their ability to take part in such an interaction is partly an index of their adjustment, but in turn it leads to a more complete adjustment, since the bereaved or divorced person begins to see himself in a new light, as an eligible partner, or simply as a man or woman rather than as the former spouse of So-and-so. In work relations, too, the individual finds that both kin and friends are unwilling to keep alive the old set of relationships and are oriented toward the present or the future. Each person must nurse his own grief and hurt within himself, and with time fewer and fewer people wish to share it.

As a consequence, in the relatively free courtship market of the United States, well over 90 per cent of those who lose a spouse by death or divorce will eventually remarry, if this occurs between roughly the ages of 20 and 35.

100

Children and Family Dissolution

What happens to the children when the family breaks up? A precise answer to this question is not possible at present, if we take seriously the differences in role patterns among the various types of family dissolutions sketched at the beginning of this chapter. Clearly, children reared in a happy home are more likely to grow up happy and psychologically healthy themselves. However, children from the "empty shell" family are not, even though no divorce has occurred. Studies of family dissolution have generally focused merely on the differences between children of divorce and other children, but so gross a comparison fails to ascertain the central facts—i.e., how adequately the various members of the family perform their role obligations to one another.

Indeed, we cannot even know how many children are involved each year in these various forms of family dissolution, since we do not know how many cases of each occur. During 1955 about 343,000 minor children were involved in divorce and annullment cases; and about 350,000 children were orphaned that year. At about the same time, mid-1955, there were "3.3 million children under age eighteen, or 5.9 per cent of the total population, whose parents had been divorced, and only 2.7 million orphans." [4] Thus about 6 million minor children had to adjust to these main forms of marital disorganization at that period.

Psychiatric studies emphasize the difficulties experienced by people who as children lived in "empty shell" families, in which people carry out their formal duties toward one another, but give no understanding, affection, or support, and have little interest in communicating with one another. Recent research has begun to uncover the destructive effects, especially on an elder sister, when a child who is severely mentally retarded is kept in the family.[5] Similarly chaotic consequences may result when a child or parent becomes psychotic.

These various categories suggest, by their complexity and potential severity, that many superficially intact homes may have an unhealthy impact on the children; and that many homes with only one parent may be relatively successful in producing healthy and happy children.

Without the necessary data, then, the question cannot be adequately answered. One type of inquiry does underline the need for more meaningful categories in our information on what happens to children when the home breaks up. Many studies have shown that delinquency is associated with "*broken* homes." Part of this link is created by the fact that divorce and mortality rates are higher in slum areas, where delinquency rates are also higher. The association may, then, be partly spurious.

Another element in this link is the failure of adequate socialization: The missing parent cannot be an adequate role model for the children, or serve as an added source of authority in enforcing conformity to social rules. This latter failure would occur, of course, whether the marriage were broken by death or by divorce.

In any event, if the class position of parents is held constant, delinquency rates *are* higher for broken than for unbroken homes, and higher for children of homes broken by separation or divorce than for homes broken by the death of a parent. This difference would be expected, because of the help and social support the bereaved person receives, and the lesser likelihood that the children

---

[4] Paul H. Jacobson, *American Marriage and Divorce* (New York: Rinehart, 1959), pp. 129, 135.

[5] Bernard Farber, *Family Organization and Crisis*, Society for Research in Child Development (Indiana), (1960), Serial No. 75, Vol. 25, No. 1.

who have lost a parent by death have lived through a period of dissension, quarreling, or problems of identification or loyalty.

However, parents who learn these facts cannot *decide* successfully to live harmoniously with one another. Almost everyone would create a happy home if he could. Their real choice is whether to continue to live together in disharmony, or to divorce. What are the consequences for the children of *these* choices?

As mentioned earlier, the data are not clear, but one important body of information suggests that "separation," which usually means that parents continue to interact unhappily with one another but avoid divorce, may be more conducive to juvenile delinquency than divorce itself.

The Gluecks related juvenile delinquency to several types of broken homes. Delinquents are slightly more likely to come from divorced homes than from intact homes. However, children from widowed or widowered homes are almost 50 per cent more likely to be delinquent than those from intact homes. But children from "separated" homes are overrepresented *still more:* The chance that such homes will produce a juvenile delinquent (holding class constant) is almost twice as high as the likelihood that an intact home will produce a juvenile delinquent.[6]

It seems likely that role failure within the home has a more destructive impact on children than the withdrawal of one spouse. In another study it was ascertained that adolescents with problems of personal adjustment were more likely to be from homes with continued marital conflict or separation than from homes broken by divorce or death.[7]

[6] Sheldon and Eleanor Glueck, *Unraveling Juvenile Delinquency* (Cambridge: Harvard University Press, 1950), Table VIII-19, p. 91.

[7] Paul H. Landis, "The Broken Home in Teenage Adjustments," *Rural Sociology Series on the Family*, No. 4 (Pullman, Washington: Institute of Agricultural Sciences, State College of Washington, 1953), p. 10.

changes
in family patterns
ten

Perhaps the oldest question in social science is, "How did things get to be the way they are today?" Yet this may also be the most difficult question to answer, since even now there is no scientifically acceptable body of theory about social change. Social change is the least developed area of sociological theory. This chapter will not, therefore, contain a theory of family change. Instead, it will attempt to clarify some of the problems in this area, and to analyze some actual processes involved in recent changes in various family systems.

A theory of social change seeks to formulate or locate patterned or *determinate* sequences of change. A mere chronology of events is not such a theory. After all, a succession of daily newspapers offers a description of social events, along with some connections between them, and moreover contains much of the raw material for such a theory; but it does not predict a series of related social processes. Certain rough sequences in the development of *non*-social objects might be determinate. For example, the wheel must come before the automobile; the ameba before the echinoderm or flatworm. Is it true, however, that matriliny or polyandry must come before patriliny or polygyny? Or low divorce rates before high ones? Or short engagements before long ones? And can we move from such crude before-after queries to sequences of *several* patterns, such as Murdock's theory of the linked steps by which the "Normal Dakota" kinship nomenclature is transformed into the "Duo-Iroquois"? [1]

The task, then, is not just to discover that certain social patterns *did* happen before others, but that such a sequence is determinate, caused by social forces which we can understand and predict. Such a goal is far too grandiose for contemporary sociology. Possibly it is not to be taken seriously as an immediate aspiration, either. Cosmogony, the study of the origins and developmental stages of stars and planets, remains the least rigorous field of astrophysics. The life cycle in plants and animals has been meticulously charted by biologists, but the result is many descriptions without rigorous theory. Perhaps the best that sociology can do is to chart numerous longer-term changes, and to interpret them as well as possible with existing generalizations about social interaction.

At present, our task is to ascertain how various social forces change family patterns, and how these may in turn affect other areas of social action.

Let us consider some problems of method and proof. First, one traditional question must be eliminated as being impossible to answer—the *origins* of the family. Even if we could penetrate the obscurities of history, we would gain data on only the last few instants of human experience in the family. Some species of man began a million years ago; *homo sapiens* certainly appeared as early as 50,000 years ago, and possibly 100,000 years ago. We have *no data at all* on family patterns of that time, and because no traces remain we shall never know what they were. The family patterns of the four great anthropoids, because they are not founded on a *cultural* system, yield only dim clues to an understanding of man's family origins, in part because they branched off the main human evolutionary line so long ago.

Second, no amount of scientific knowledge enables us to predict precisely the future outcome of any present situation, whether physical or social. A concrete situation is the nexus of many kinds of forces, while each science confines its predictions to a small number of variables only, ignoring the rest. The physical sciences could not predict the *exact* course of future lava flow down a mountainside, and the much less developed field of sociology cannot predict the specific family future of Mr. Brown, or the exact future of the Western family system. At best, we can assert, on the basis of well-founded social regularities, some of the forms it will *not* take, and a few likely possibilities. In addition, of course, we can achieve greater predictive accuracy, the shorter the time interval. We could predict, for example, with almost no chance of being proved incorrect, that the Western family system will not be measurably different next week from what it is today.

Factors in Family Change

It follows from the preceding discussion that what are called "theories of social or family change" are not that at all, but are unifactorial hypotheses—that is, they assert that family or social change has been shaped or caused primarily by one great factor, such as race, climate, or economics.

A common notion among social scientists, for example, is that technological or industrial change is *the* great factor in family change. Such hypotheses derive their strength from a common-sense plausibility: Clearly, family life *is* different in industrial England from life in Stone Age Australia. They are additionally persuasive, because the global causal factor in fact encompasses nearly everything; since it *is* everything, naturally it causes everything. "Industrialization," like "urbanization," is made to include not merely machines, but the science and engineering that produced them; the secular attitudes of the

---

[1] George P. Murdock, *Social Structure* (New York: Macmillan, 1949), p. 251.

changes in family patterns

modern era; anti-traditionalism in certain areas; job placement on the basis of competence; an open-class system; high geographical mobility—in short, all the traits that set off this particular epoch in Western history. Industrialization in this vague but enveloping sense does "cause" the modern social and family patterns, but only because it is identical with them. Such an hypothesis is true, but trivial.

To transform such a truism into a worthwhile exploratory probe we must discover which *elements* of industrialism first enter a society, and precisely what are the points of impact of those elements on various sectors of family life.

Such an inquiry demands that we first concede how universal are social and family change. Analysts frequently refer to a tribe as having lived out its family patterns "unchanged for thousands of years until white men came." No such assertion has ever been proved. Informants in isolated societies usually claim that "in the old days" all family behavior was clearly understood, and everyone obeyed. No such period, however, has ever been documented. The claim must rather be seen as a mode of social control by which the old persuade the young of the correctness of traditional ways.

Very likely, if we were able to interview people in any society at any time in the past, they would grant that social patterns had indeed changed *recently*, but would insist that in their grandfathers' day things had not changed from the ancient and rightful ways of old. The theme of bemoaning the rapid pace of modern change, as against the harmonious, unaltered family behavior of the past, is an old one.

The study of family change is especially plagued by the prevalence of myths about the past. Most discussions of the U.S. family contain such a myth, which typically depicts a harmonious life down on grandmother's self-sufficient farm. Whether this myth corresponds to reality, we do not know, since very little historical research has attempted to test it. Not a single history of the U.S. family would meet modern standards of historical research.[2]

Problems in Analyzing Family Change

There are formidable technical problems involved in analyzing the family behavior of the past, since most family events do not ordinarily leave traces in the form of laws, documents, or treaties, much less systematic continuous records. Formal events such as births, deaths, marriages, divorces, adoptions, and lawsuits about inheritance are likely to be recorded, but these yield only few insights into family patterns. The comments of literary or philosophical figures about their times are at best the guesses of wise but untrained amateurs. Moreover, both records and comments focus on the top social strata only, leaving nearly in obscurity the family behavior of the majority of the population.

Faced with these handicaps, we must adopt a skeptical stance with reference to most of our assumptions about how the family changed in the past. Specifically, we can measure change only if we have a secure base point, and thus we must be careful to ascertain that point with some precision. We can demonstrate that the U.S. divorce rate has been rising for a century, because we have data from that earlier base point. We cannot, however, prove that family life was much more harmonious a century ago, or people more contented in it. Both hypotheses may be correct, but we do not have an adequate description of family life at that time to measure how much it has changed since then.

[2] Even if we confine ourselves to narrow time periods, the excellent study of Edmund S. Morgan, *The Puritan Family* (Boston: Boston Public Library, 1944), has almost no counterpart for other epochs.

It cannot be assumed, either, that if we can measure one type of family change—e.g., the illegitimacy rate—that other family behavior is changing at the same rate. In fact, a good sociological guess would be to the contrary. For some existing family patterns are under great strain, while others may resist strongly a new social pressure. An example of the former was the deference and service due to the Chinese mother-in-law from her daughter-in-law under the Ch'ing Dynasty. The socially predictable alliance between a young groom and his bride, as against his elders, was held in check by a number of factors. The young man was dependent economically on his male elders, and rebellion against them would arouse disapproval by a wide range of kin and friends. He was not permitted to be alone with his wife except at night, or to show affection to her even when with his relatives. Too close an emotional tie between the young groom and bride might cause the bride to be sent back to her family. She could not, on the other hand, oppose his kin, since no one would have supported her, not even her husband.

However, in the generation following the downfall in 1911 of the Chinese Empire, and still more intensively over the period since World War II under the impact of Communist ideology, the rule of elders has been widely attacked. The male elders no longer exert economic control over their young relatives, and the clan has nearly disappeared. The mother-in-law is not likely to live with the young couple, and they are now permitted to fall in love with each other before they marry. Consequently, young brides felt less constrained to follow the old custom which young brides did not like even under the traditional system. That is, the pattern was always under considerable strain, and under modern conditions its various supports have been removed.

By contrast, the very close emotional tie between mother and son in India has not been subjected to any ideological attack, was not under great strain under the traditional system, and is not exposed to much undermining pressure in the modern generation. Consequently, we would not expect much change in the intensity of this relationship in the near future.

The foregoing analysis of central problems in any theory of family change suggests why the few such theories that have been entertained over the past century have not been adequate. Social science has developed but one comprehensive theory of family change, based on nineteenth-century evolutionism, and has discarded it without being able to develop a satisfactory substitute. It was a reconstruction of the past, erected on deductions from supposed "survivals"— i.e., modern family customs or kinship nomenclatures that were assumed to be evidence (as a sort of social fossil) about the past.

For example, in many societies the groom and his party must engage in a mock battle in which they tear the bride away from her kin and carry her off to join the groom. From this custom it was deduced that in the distant past brides were obtained by capture. No one seems to have pointed out that if a group actually succeeded in kidnapping a young woman, they did not have to marry her at all, but could use her in any way they chose. Similarly, by studying Australian aborigines or Polynesians, we could presumably learn about Stone Age family customs, since each technological stage was correlated with a specific family stage.

The core of this speculative edifice was the notion, then, that with each step forward in technology man also "advanced" in religious and familial behavior. With reference to the family, it was believed that man had progressed from sexual promiscuity in a semi-animal horde, to matriarchy, then to patri-archy of a polygynous type, finally to achieve the highest spiritual pinnacle, Victorian monogamy. This reconstruction was not so much destroyed by contrary

changes in family patterns

evidence as it was ignored, because under the new standards of evidence in the early twentieth century it was without real support. No trace of any actual system of promiscuity has been found, nor any matriarchal system. Clear correlations between technological level and family system also failed to appear. And, as noted before, the Australian aborigines were finally seen to be as distant as modern Europeans from Neolithic or Eolithic man.

The Marxian theory became intertwined with this reconstruction largely through the work of Engels (who based his evolutionary ideas on the research of the American anthropologist, Morgan), but Marx himself focused his empirical inquiry on the changes in the British family under the impact of the factory. Since the machine can do the work of the human hand, it can be multiplied or speeded up. Substituting for the skilled hand, it can be operated by women and children. Consequently, almost all members of the family can work, and wages can be reduced to the level where all *must* work to survive. Since the capital costs of the machine continue whether it operates or stands idle, it is most efficient to run it long hours. Consequently, the factory owner must hire the cheapest labor, and work his labor as hard as possible, if he is not to be squeezed out of business by less squeamish competitors.

Marx summarized the results from numerous empirical inquiries conducted by the investigating commissions of his day. Women and children were put to work, mother and child were separated, and children were neglected. Mortality rates of infants and children rose. Fathers sold their children's labor, and sometimes in effect their children, on harsh terms.[3] Young girls had no opportunity to learn the arts of housekeeping. The factory system, driven by the impulse to maximize profit, undermined the traditional lower-class family organization.

The actual processes of development from the late eighteenth through the first half of the nineteenth century seem to have been somewhat more complex. In the earlier phases of the factory system, men could supervise their own children within the factory, and thus retain their paternal authority. Later on, this authority waned as newer types of machinery were introduced, and then resentment against the factory began to rise.

Of course, the British family system did not continue to disintegrate. On the other hand, Marx had not aimed at a generalized theory of family change; his philosophical position, derived from Hegel, assumed that social-scientific interpretations were valid only for particular events or epochs, in this case the rise of the capitalist system.

One other theory of family change should be mentioned, the Marxian-inspired theory of William F. Ogburn. In his early work Ogburn asserted that the prime mover of social change is technology ("material culture") and that the non-material elements adjust to it after a time ("culture lag"), but his actual research and his later theoretical position were more eclectic. He saw a wide range of new elements as sources of family change, from ideologies to airplanes. Like many family analysts of the past generation, he saw the modern family as "losing its functions," because industrial production took place in factories, education in schools, religious training in churches, and so on. This view of family change is rather vague in meaning, and for the most part is simply an incorrect statement of what has been taking place.

Ogburn's "theory" is a general approach rather than a set of linked hypotheses, and simply directs us to look for the origins of family change in specific

[3] A good example of his data and reasoning may be found in *Capital* (N.Y.: Modern Library, 1936), Chap. XV.

technological innovations (consider, for example, how the automobile frees individuals from family controls). He evaluated this connection by common-sense rather than by rigorous research design, and took for granted that engineering innovations would be accepted on the grounds of rationality. As against this looseness, however, he was careful to prove false a number of assumptions about changes in the family. For example, the average size of the U.S. household did decrease from 1850 to 1950 (5.5 to 3.5 persons, but obviously the swarming, multi-family household of myth was not common even a century ago. Similarly, he summarized research data to show that the "labor-saving devices" of the U.S. home had not reduced the number of hours the housewife worked each week.

Industrialization and the Family

Family research in the post-World War II period has documented one gross empirical regularity whose processes are not yet clearly understood—that in all parts of the world and for the first time in world history all social systems are moving fast or slowly toward some form of the conjugal family system and also toward industrialization. In agreement with the intuition of social analysts for over a century is the finding that with industrialization the traditional family systems—usually, extended or joint family systems, with or without lineages or clans—are breaking down. On the other hand, since each system begins from a somewhat different base point, the direction of change in any given family pattern may be different. The divorce rate has been dropping for half a century in Japan, and for a shorter period in certain Arab countries (e.g., Algeria), but has been rising in Western countries. The age at marriage has been dropping in most Western countries, but rising in India, the Arab countries, and (among women) in sub-Sahara Africa, yet all are moving toward some form of the conjugal system.

Earlier, as seen in Chapter 5, structural characteristics of the conjugal family system were outlined, most of them derivable from its lesser extension of kinship relations. These traits fit rather well the demands of industrialization.[4] Under the industrial system, the individual is supposed to be hired because of his competence, and in promotion the same standards are to be applied to all who hold the same job (i.e., the standards are achievement-based and universalistic). His relationship to the job is also functionally specific—i.e., his role obligations are confined to getting the task done. Put another way, the extended family system, with its standards of ascription, particularism, and diffuseness, is ideally not permitted to interfere with the efficient functioning of a modern enterprise.

Because of its emphasis on performance, such a system requires that a person be permitted to rise or fall, and to move about wherever the job market is best. A lesser emphasis on land ownership also increases the ease of mobility. The conjugal family system is neolocal (each couple sets up its own household), and its kinship network is not strong, thus putting fewer barriers than other family systems in the way of class or geographical mobility.

In these ways the conjugal family system "fits" the needs of industrialism. But the relationship may also be put another way. Since increasingly an industrializing society—consider, for example, the Arab countries, or India—creates formal agencies to handle the major tasks of any kinship groupings larger than the nuclear family, such units as lineages, clans, or even large extended families also lose their functions and thereby the *allegiance* they once commanded.

---

[4] For a more extended analysis of this problem, see William J. Goode, *World Revolution and Family Patterns* (New York: The Free Press of Glencoe, 1963), Chap. I.

changes in family patterns

Thus individual families go their own way, ignoring such extended kinship ties.

More important, elders no longer control the major new economic or political opportunities, so that family authority slips from the hands of such family leaders. The young groom can obtain his bride price on his own, and need not concern himself about the good will of his elders. The couple need not obey any one outside their family unit, since only their performance on the job is relevant for their advancement. They need not even rely on family elders for job instruction, since schools, the factory, or the plantation or mine will teach them the new skills. Nor do they even need to continue working on the land, still in the possession of the elders, since the jobs and political opportunities are in the city. Thus industrialization is likely to undermine gradually the traditional systems of family control and exchange. The terms of the role-bargaining between the generations have been altered.

It is with reference to this set of links that the preceding chapter on stratification analyzed the concentration of controls in the hands of upper-strata families. When Western societies underwent industrialization, the new opportunities remained in the hands of middle- or upper-class families who owned these new enterprises. Thus their bargaining power might be reduced under the new system, but not so much as that of lower-class families. By contrast, upper-strata native families in newly conquered regions, were apt to lose *more* than families toward the lower strata. Thus, after the initial period of conquest, the indigenous tribal leaders were removed in the New World. The Spanish and Portugese rulers took all the important positions and opportunities. Native rulers lost control over their families and their political authority collapsed. Most often, however, the European empire builders have tried to rule *through* the tribal leaders, yielding few chances for economic or political advancement to the young natives, *independent* of their elders. Thus, these leaders would not lose control over their sons. On the other hand, as a larger percentage of the tribe or society is drawn into the new economic enterprises and is hired and promoted on its own merits, the leaders of large kinship groupings do lose their ability to elicit obedience to traditional family customs.

The conjugal emphasis on emotionality within the family also serves somewhat the needs of industrialism. At lower job levels, the worker experiences little intrinsic job satisfaction; at higher levels, he obtains more job satisfaction, but is also subject to rather great demands. At any level, the enterprise has no responsibility for the emotional input-output balance of the individual; this is solely the responsibility of the family, in the sense that there is nowhere else to go for it. The small family, then, deals with a problem which the industrial system cannot handle.

The "Fit" between Industrialism and the Conjugal Family

Nevertheless, we cannot, in analyzing the interaction of the great social forces making for family change, presume some sort of natural "harmony" between the modern complex of industrialism and the conjugal family system. Both are unplanned resultants of individual desires and initiatives. Both are systems of forces, each with its own needs, and at various points either may fail to serve the needs of the other. To place everyone in his job solely on the basis of merit, for example, would require the destruction of the family system entirely. On the other hand, without a family unit to deal with the idiosyncrasies of aged parents, the emotional needs of adults, or the insecurities of children, very likely not enough adequately functioning people would be produced to man the industrial system.

This is another way of reasserting a central notion of this volume, that family and industrial factors or variables are *independent* but interacting. Neither fully determines the other, although both influence each other. Consequently, we cannot assume, in looking for patterns of family change, that industrial forces shape everything (unless we *define* them as including everything) to their measure. The very *resistance* of family systems to such pressures indicates their independence as a set of forces, even if the massive political and economic changes ultimately outweigh that resistance.

Since we have analyzed some of the ways in which family systems have altered to serve the needs of industrialization, we should also consider briefly how an industrial system fails to handle some of the problems created by this change toward a conjugal family system. Thereafter, we shall discuss two other types of relationships of social change (1) the resistance of family patterns to change, and (2) how a family system may facilitate industrialization.

The neolocal, independent household and its accompanying values in favor of separate lives for each couple leave the old parents in an ambiguous position. Some elements in this situation we commented on earlier—e.g., the sudden displacement of the older male from his job, the lack of land as a basis for social status, the relative unimportance of wisdom as compared with specialized technical knowledge, and the inability of the old to control the economic or social opportunities offered to young adults. In 1962 there were about 17 million people in the United States aged 65 years and over, about 9 per cent of the population, and this segment will increase in size in the future. Every study of their situation shows that they need help, although there is disagreement over where the help should come from. People no longer accept without question an obligation to care for the old, especially in a common household.

Similarly, the obligation to rear orphan children of relatives is not so definite as in the past. Modern society has, of course, invented various procedures for locating and evaluating both foster and step-parents for such children, as well as continuing until recently the older system of orphanges; but the action of the state does not fully substitute for the active kinship system of a primitive society.

In a parallel way, as noted earlier, the modern conjugal system does not adequately deal with the structural disruptions caused by divorce.

Modern industrialism has offered women more economic freedom, but has not relieved them of their household tasks. Labor-saving devices merely raise the standards of cleanliness and general performance, permitting more work to be turned out, but do not reduce the hours of work. The primary status of women in all societies is that of housekeeper and mother, so that in spite of higher levels of technical training, women have not developed a commensurately high level of career-mindedness over the past half-century in Western countries. Indeed, toward the higher social strata, where more women are better educated, a lower percentage of women are in the labor force, but apparently a *higher* percentage would like to be. The modern egalitarianism within the family means that the man's energies are somewhat diverted into helping at household tasks, away from his job demands.

Industrialization and Fertility

An especially complex and important set of relations in family change may be found in worldwide efforts to reduce the birth rate in nations undergoing industrialization. In all but the highly industrialized societies, fertility is accorded high priority, but the ranks of the living are depleted by death. A high mortality rate, especially among its young people, is a heavy economic burden for a society to bear: The society invests physical maintenance for a time, but they do not live long enough to repay it. The industrial society, by contrast, develops the scientific knowledge necessary to reduce mortality, which increases further its productive efficiency.[5]

From the earliest period of socialization in most societies, the child is told that eventually he will marry and produce children. Usually, the full privileges of adulthood are not conceded until the individual has produced children. Great effort is expended to inculcate fertility values in everyone. This extensive cultural apparatus, designed to make fertility very much a part of the individual's personality needs, is in sharp contrast to the relative lack of cultural emphasis on an individual's taking care of his own life and avoiding death. Death is an intimately personal affair, and apparently human beings need very little special socialization to try to avoid it. The obligation of producing other persons, to whom we shall owe extensive and burdensome obligations, requires considerable social reinforcement.

This emphasis is necessary for the survival of the less industrialized, high mortality societies. The adjustive controls in the social structure—abortion or infanticide—come *after* conception. This relative emphasis insures quick replacement if the population is sharply reduced by war, epidemics, or famine. It would not be possible suddenly to institute a set of high fertility values as an adjustment, since this kind of socialization would take a generation to have any important effect. On the other hand, to the extent that everyone in the society strongly favors fertility, and has a set of personality needs that are satisfied only by high fertility, it is difficult for a society quickly to take up some contraceptive pattern when mortality is suddenly reduced and the population begins to grow faster than the increase in productive capacity. In several countries since World War II, the death rate has been reduced by 25 to 50 per cent within the span of 2 or 3 years, but with no reduction in the birth rate.

The interaction of these factors creates a special problem for the modern era—the world's population explosion. Most societies can now be classified as either high growth societies, or high potential growth societies. That is, either their birth rate is already much higher than their death rate, or their birth rate is high and their death rate is in the process of being reduced by modern scientific techniques.

This situation arises, as noted, from the difference between the kinds of actions needed for decreasing mortality rates, as against those required to reduce birth rates. To reduce mortality rates, the leaders of a society require no more than a modicum of cooperation from the bulk of the population. A clean water supply can be introduced, or a more effective sewerage system, without a vote or without any individual decisions by those effected. Pesticides can almost wipe out one of man's great killers, malaria, without much help on the part of individuals. To lower mortality to the rates found in industrial societies does of course require learning new habits. However, very great reductions in mortality can take place without much cooperation. In any event, cooperation seems not to be difficult to obtain, since people can be readily convinced that modern medicine and science can save their lives, and this is a goal desired by all.

To lower the birth rate, on the other hand, requires a change in a family pattern, an alteration in *individual* goals. Conception is an intimately personal matter, not a mass phenomenon.

[5] An especially good analysis of these relations may be found in Kingsley Davis and Judith Blake, "Social Structure and Fertility," *Economic Development and Social Change* (April 1956), 211–235.

Since the socialization of all individuals has emphasized the importance of fertility, the attempt to lower birth rates requires an important shift in the attitudes, habits, and values of individuals relative to their family roles. Indeed the situation raises the recurrent sociological question, How much can family custom be changed by conscious plan? The use of contraception is costly, and requires much discipline. In addition, although modern religious leaders in Japan, Islam, and India have gradually come to assert that their doctrines do not specifically prohibit the use of contraception, in fact until recently the main thrust of most great religious systems had been against the use of contraception, whether in Western nations, India, or China. In India a son was required to perform certain rituals upon his father's death, else the father would not be able to assume a new form in a subsequent life. The Chinese emphasis upon the unbroken link between ancestors and the living again urged a relatively high fertility. Until the 1950's the religious leaders of Islam claimed that Islamic doctrine was against the use of contraception. On the other hand, population control was relatively easily introduced in Japan, where family limitation had been common for generations.

In our own society, where the birth rate presently is well over one-third higher than that of Japan, we pity those who have not had children. Women who have had an involuntary abortion often suffer from a feeling of inadequacy if this was their first conception. Those who cannot have children often feel driven to adopt one.

Sex Roles and Fertility

Sex roles also affect fertility and the possibility of reducing it. At the present time, research projects are under way in every major nation of the world in an effort to ascertain the detailed factors which lead to conception, and these projects have been especially aimed at uncovering the variables which produce a high birth rate in less industrialized countries where a high rate of reproduction increases the population faster than the economic productive capacity increases. Let us look at a particular case, that of Puerto Rico.

Puerto Rico illustrates two points of some consequence here. One is that high fertility in the population at large is not any individual's particular *motivation*. Those who have many children had no special desire to keep the birth rate up or to lower it. Second, the motivations that do induce a large number of children continue to be inculcated long after the point in history when high fertility might be useful to the society.

The Puerto Rican family typically "spoils" its male children, as judged by Western standards. The appropriate relation between a husband and his wife is not one in which the man exhibits tenderness or expresses his true inner feelings to the woman, or exposes his personal weaknesses and needs. Instead he must play the role of being dominant, powerful, and *macho* (masculine). Although achievement of an intellectual or occupational character becomes increasingly important, these cannot substitute at all for the male qualities of violence, courage, and virility, especially at lower-class levels where intellectual or occupational achievement is unlikely anyway. The young male's early sex experiences are likely to be with a prostitute, since young girls are guarded rather carefully. These factors mean that there is always a communication and role barrier between husband and wife, which prevent either from really understanding each other, especially with respect to sex and contraception.

Machismo is a quality which must be proved continually. The man may

112

not rest on his laurels. In the sexual area this means that he must be sexually able, and in the reproductive area that he must continue to produce children to prove his masculinity. This is especially necessary, since so many men have little opportunity of rising in the occupational sphere. Here again is one area where the male can continue to be dominant and powerful. The woman, by contrast, can prove her maternal qualities by producing as few as one child or two. The evidence of her womanly role behavior remains as the children continue to grow. As a consequence, then, men usually oppose contraceptives, even when having children may be financially ruinous. He views their use as a discipline that he does not wish to submit to, as ego-destructive. Notice that this set of factors is not specifically Roman Catholic in origin, although of course the Church does oppose contraceptives. In fact, there is considerable anti-clericalism in Puerto Rican society. In one study of fertility in Puerto Rico,[6] a higher percentage of men than of women wanted any given number of children above the number of two. The same relationship held when the respondents were asked what was the ideal number of children their daughters should have. This attitude extends to other areas as well. For example, 28 per cent of the men, but 46 per cent of the women, approved of women working.

One interesting result in this particular case is that since men do not bother about contraceptives and indeed oppose them, women seek to learn how to prevent babies, and most utilize techniques that do not depend on the man's desire or discipline. Since most of the factors in the family structure of Puerto Rico press toward early sexual relations and conception, women have increasingly turned to sterilization as one possible solution.

The evidence from many studies in different parts of the world parallels that in Puerto Rico in at least one particular, that women are much less inclined to have a large number of children than men are, and that above a certain number of children (the number varying with the society) a majority of women actually are in favor of using some type of birth control. Typically, as in our own country, the lower classes are less inclined to utilize contraceptives. Notice that even in our own country, men have far less mistrust of the contraceptives they use than women do.

It must be emphasized, however, that we are far from understanding the psychological and social factors which change the social definition of the appropriate size of family. The complexity of this problem became evident after World War II. Prior to that time in the industrial Western countries there had been a steady long term decline in fertility. The assumption of demographers was that this pattern would continue after World War II, though it was anticipated that immediately after the war there would be the usual rise in the birth rate. When hostilities ceased, as is well known, the birth rate did rise, but remained high in many countries. In most, by now, the birth rate has dropped again. It has already begun to drop somewhat in the United States, but meanwhile the absolute rate remains high (about 22 births per 1,000 population each year) and it is much higher than in most other Western countries.

Research now going on in all class levels seeks to uncover the social and cultural factors that maintain so high a rate. A simple economic interpretation of such family changes will not suffice. In general, fertility rates rise in Western nations as we descend the social scale, but within each class division, those with more income will be somewhat more fertile. Moreover, if a simple eco-

[6] Paul K. Hatt, *Backgrounds of Human Fertility in Puerto Rico* (Princeton: Princeton University Press, 1952).

nomic interpretation were applicable, then few or no parents would have many children, since under modern circumstances they never represent a profit. Viewed in purely economic terms, children are a burden.

On the other hand, one element of the economic interpretation appears to apply, since no nation seems to have a *low* infant mortality rate for long without moving toward a low birth rate. That is to say, when nearly all infants have a long life expectancy, the family adjusts to this fact by having fewer children. Present efforts in every major industrializing country to lower infant mortality and to introduce contraceptives will presumably succeed, over the next generation, in altering this resistant family pattern.

Effect of the Family on Industrialization

Let us now consider another relationship between family factors and social change, the possibility that the family system may have an independent, facilitating effect on the modern shift toward industrialization.

No full-scale research into this hypothesis has been carried out, but a few suggestive facts may be noted here. Negatively, of course, many observers have pointed out that extended and joint family systems prevented a free utilization of talent as well as the easy introduction of innovations against the power and traditionalism of family elders. Positively, it should be kept in mind that the family systems of the West have been different from those of other major civilizations for over a thousand years. Child or early adolescent marriage was not the ideal or the statistically usual. There was no ancestor worship, and *individuals*, not families, were responsible for crimes. There was no lineage or clan system, and the eldest male was not necessarily the leader of the family. Young couples were expected to live independently, for the most part.

Moreover, these differences were accentuated when the individualistic, anti-traditional ideology of ascetic Protestantism began to spread. The Puritans in the U.S., for example, defined husband and wife as loving companions rather than simply part of a family network, and their children had more freedom of marital choice than was possible in the traditional European family systems. Divorce became possible, even though disapproved. It seems likely by the time the new factory jobs opened in the late eighteenth century in England that the family system of at least part of the population was in some harmony with its new demands. Their extended kinship ties and obligations, and their links with family land, did not interfere with the new type of work obligations.

A more striking instance of the importance of family patterns in facilitating or hindering social change may be found in the contrast between the success of Japan and China in their attempt to industrialize during the late nineteenth and early twentieth centuries.[7]

Both were opened to the West at about the same time, and both faced a somewhat similar set of problems: threat of conquest, an agrarian economy, a rapid growth of population, extensive bureaucracies that had become corrupt and inefficient, an emphasis on familism not individualism, strains between town and country, and the low prestige of merchants, who would have to assume important roles in any modernizing process.

As against China's essential failure to cope with its problems, within

---

[7] Marion J. Levy, "Contrasting Factors in the Modernization of China and Japan," in Simon S. Kuznets, Wilbert E. Moore, and Joseph J. Spengler (eds.), *Economic Growth: Brazil, India, Japan* (Durham, N.C.: Duke University Press, 1955).

changes in family patterns

about half a century after 1868 Japan had established heavy industries with almost no outside capital, altered its system of distribution, made both male and female literacy almost universal, and introduced a new set of social relationships, characteristic of the Western market system.

Several differences between the Japanese and Chinese family systems contributed to their varying successes in coping with the problems of industrialization. One was the pattern of inheritance. Under the Chinese family system, all sons inherited equally, so that family capital could not usually be kept intact. In Japan one son (usually the oldest) inherited all the property. Thus wealth could be accumulated, and one person could more easily make a decision to invest it.

Perhaps the most important family differences lay in the relationship between family and state. In China the personal loyalty was owed to the Emperor, but not if conflicted with family loyalty. A man owed his first duty to his father, and through him to clan elders. Being unfilial was the greatest of Chinese sins. Of course, the Japanese man owed loyalty to his father, but the system was *feudalistic* rather than familistic: An unbroken chain of fealty linked each individual through his father and his father's leader or lord, through successively higher ranks to the great princes and the Emperor. Orders from above were backed by family pressure. The radical alterations which the Meiji leaders tried to implement called for much sacrifice—for example, former warriors might be put to work, or used as policemen—but the links of fealty between family and family, and family and state, remained strong.

The Chinese regarded nepotism as a duty. A man could not reject his family if he improved his station in life, and he was expected to carry upward with him as many members as he could. In Japan social mobility was more difficult. Ideally, in contrast to China, people should remain in their places. However, *adoption* was one important mode of social ascent in Japan. A father might even disinherit a son in order to adopt a talented young man. However, the individual so chosen rose alone. He became part of the new family, and was no longer a member of his old family. Both in fact and predisposition this pattern favored innovations under the Meiji leaders: (1) the Japanese were somewhat less handicapped by nepotism, (2) those who rose did not need to help the undeserving members of his family of birth, and (3) men could seek out talented young men for placement in positions of opportunity.

One long-term family process also lowered the capacity of the Chinese to meet the problems of the new era. Since both in fact and ideal the Chinese system permitted social mobility, but accorded the merchant a lowly social rank, a common mobility path was to acquire wealth through commerce, but then to leave that occupation. The gentry were landowners and scholars. Those who acquired wealth sought to achieve prestige and power by becoming members of the gentry or training their sons to become members. The humanistic learning of the mandarins was essentially irrelevant to the problems of the modern era. Thus there was no steady accumulation of a technical and financial tradition by the successful families. By contrast, the Japanese merchant was confined to a narrower type of mobility: financial success. He had little chance of moving out of commerce and into high social ranks. But as a consequence, Japanese merchants and banking families had developed a considerable technical knowledge and tradition and were much better prepared to cope with the complex financial problems that accompanied the rapid industrialization of Japan during the Meiji period.

It must be emphasized that these cases are extremely complex, and family variables cannot be said to be the prime creators of the dramatic contrast. Nevertheless, it seems clear that they did make an important contribution to the striking differences in the industrial achievement of the two countries.

The importance of the family as a unit in the social mobility system, and thus as a facilitating element in social change, may also be seen in another major historical event, the French Revolution. This connection was commented on in the chapter on stratification. Some bourgeois families had moved into the nobility in the seventeenth and eighteenth centuries, as they had moved into the gentry in China, by acquiring wealth and beginning to live in the style of the upper stratum. This included humanistic education, or at least the support of arts and letters, fine manners, taste in clothing and furniture, and, of course, abandoning the commercial or manufacturing activities of the bourgeoisie. Those who aspired upward had to concede the superiority of the nobles, else there was no reason to move upward; but by definition, to be noble was to have been born noble. The successful bourgeois was caught in an ideological dilemma. It must be emphasized that his aim was not simply to associate with the nobility in government, or to make advantageous deals with those in power. It was rather to move his *family* and thus his family line into the nobility.

When the nobility began, over the course of the eighteenth century, to close gradually the various routes by which some bourgeois families might achieve a validation of noble status, this high stratum began to withdraw its support of the system as a whole, and instead began to view the nobility as a shackle or barrier to national progress, a violation of tenets of freedom. Moreover, the bourgeoisie furnished much of the leadership of the French Revolution in 1789.

A Concluding Comment

It is appropriate to close this little volume with the most difficult area of family analysis, the factors that produce or hinder family and social change. Thereby, we leave many central questions for future research. More important, the major theories and methodological problems in family change are relevant to all the preceding chapters. Throughout the book, allusions have been made to many relations between family variables and other social variables—divorce rates, class differentials, industrialization, the distribution of authority within the family, or the breakdown of organized descent groupings. In many of these discussions, our focus was primarily on how and why these changes were taking place. However, to analyze how and why such changes occur, we must know the causal factors that cause any determinate relations. With reference to each of these patterns, only proximate and immediate forces were suggested as causes, primarily those which change the bargaining relationship between people in different social positions (e.g., how upper-class families control their youngsters more effectively than do lower-class families).

Such causal relationships, or correlations, are far from stating determinate *sequences* of change, but they are the foundation for establishing such sequences. In any event, whether we seek such determinate changes, or simpler correlations, we meet the same difficulties in theory and method. To be avoided are all theories that turn out to be only unifactorial hypotheses, suggesting that all change and all causal relations flow from some single, global factor, such as race, environment, technology, or industrialism. In the past these seemed plausible only because analysts who proposed them usually included within such global variables almost everything that needed to be explained.

116

Nevertheless, even such global theories have some utility, since they have as one of their aims the destruction of prior theories, and thus must muster some empirical data to support this aim. The accumulation of data helps us, then, to construct more adequate explanations. We need the facts, because our experience is narrowly confined to only a few families, and we have been taught many "facts" that were not correct. Only a few years ago, it was generally agreed, for example, that toward the upper social strata the divorce rate rose; and that divorce was more likely to lead to juvenile delinquency than was any other solution to marital difficulties.

All societies develop myths about their present family systems, as well as about the past. The "adolescent rebellion" turns out to be a most modest assault on adult values, when the data are examined. Most Americans did not once live in large, rambling houses that sheltered a numerous extended family. Most Americans lived in one-room dwellings, with perhaps a cooking lean-to attached. The finer houses were more likely to survive to the present, for reasons that are obvious. We cannot assume that modern family morals are really worse than the golden past, if we read details of individual lives in, say, the eighteenth century, in Sweden, France, Italy, or England.

The steady testing of hypotheses about how family behavior is shaped will, then, help us to develop a clearer conception about both the present and the past. Perhaps we shall learn thereby much more about the reciprocal relations between family patterns and the traits of the larger society. Granted that industrialization affects the position of the wife, it seems also likely that the family system may itself affect many other social processes. For example, considerable evidence is accumulating that the socialization experiences of the boy within the family—based in turn on the structure of authority within it—may powerfully affect his later motivation to achieve, and thus the patterns of social mobility in the larger society. How family systems at different social levels utilize the economic system may shape political debate, by permitting or hindering upward mobility and thereby increasing or decreasing satisfaction with the opportunity structure.

Nevertheless, our aim in scientific work is to ascertain determinate relations, to understand the direction of causal influence, to comprehend the social process. It is not so important to prove that societal variables shape family variables, or the reverse. What is significant is to locate the prime causal relations, whatever the major variables turn out to be. The accumulation of new research data, often correcting past opinion or guess, has been progressing rapidly over the past decade. The challenge of the immediate future is both to ascertain the facts more accurately, and to develop more adequate theories to account for them.

selected references

The works noted below are useful for extending the student's acquaintance with important data about particular family systems, as well as with ideas for interpreting family behavior.

Norman W. Bell and Ezra F. Vogel, "Toward a Framework for Functional Analysis of Family Behavior," in Bell and Vogel (eds.), *The Family* (Glencoe, Ill.: The Free Press, 1960), pp. 1–33, is a thoughtful attempt to lay the groundwork for a more fruitful analysis of the family. George P. Murdock, *Social Structure* (New York: Macmillan, 1949) is a major monograph, testing many hypotheses about kinship relations.

Robert F. Winch, *Mate Selection* (New York: Harper, 1958) presents data for the theory of complementarity. The books, noted below, which deal with other cultures, also describe the process of marriage formation. John L. Thomas, "The Factor of Religion in the Selection of Marriage Mates," *American Sociological Review* (1951), 16:487–492, in Marvin Sussman, *Sourcebook in Marriage and the Family*, 2nd ed. (Boston: Houghton Mifflin, 1962), pp. 108–112, shows the extent to which "like marry like" in the United States.

Two good sourcebooks for demographic materials on the family are Paul C. Glick, *American Families* (New York: Wiley, 1957); and Paul Jacobson, *American Marriage and Divorce* (New York: Rinehart, 1959).

A comparison of premarital sexual behavior and norms focused on illegitimacy may be found in Harold T. Christenson, "Cultural Relativism and Premarital Sex Norms," *American Sociological Review* (1960), 14:31–39. An excellent framework for the study of fertility patterns is presented by Kingsley Davis and Judith Blake, "Social Structure and Fertility," *Economic Development and Social Change* (April 1956), 4:211–235, also in S. M. Lipset and Neil J. Smelser (eds.), *Sociology, the Progress of a Decade* (Englewood Cliffs, N.J.: Prentice-Hall, 1961), pp. 356–377. In *Premarital Sexual Standards in America* (Glencoe, Ill.: The Free Press, 1960), Ira Reiss contrasts the sexual behavior of Americans with their attitudes.

Talcott Parsons, *Family, Socialization, and Interaction Process* (Glencoe, Ill.: The Free Press, 1955) reformulates psychodynamic theory as a mode of interpreting family relations. William N. Stephens, *The Family in Cross-cultural Perspective* (New York: Holt, Rinehart and Winston, 1963) tests both psychological and sociological hypotheses about family relations. A good summary and analysis of the studies relating child-rearing practices to later personality patterns of the children may be found in William H. Sewell, "Social Class and Childhood Personality," *Sociometry* (1961), 24:340–355; and in Robert F. Winch, Robert McGinnis, and H. R. Barringer (eds.), *Selected Studies in Marriage and the Family*, rev. ed. (New York: Holt, Rinehart and Winston, 1962), pp. 323–339.

A collection of reports edited by F. Ivan Nye, *Working Mothers* (New York: Rand McNally, 1963) contains the most up-to-date materials on this topic. Harvey J. Locke, *Predicting Adjustment in Marriage* (New York: Holt, 1951) compares the marital adjustment of happily married and divorced couples, to ascertain the utility of a Burgess-Cottrell type of marital-adjustment questionnaire.

Most full descriptions of a family system deal with stratification, but special attention should be given to Elinor G. Barber, *The Bourgeoisie in 18th Century France* (Princeton: Princeton University Press, 1955) and S. C. Dube, *Indian Village* (London: Routledge and Kegan Paul, 1955). Robert K. Merton, "Intermarriage and the Social Structure," *Psychiatry* (1941), 4:361–374, analyzes the effect of both race and class on the mating patterns of the United States.

Larger kinship structures such as the lineage are a primary focus of attention in David M. Schneider and E. Kathleen Gough (eds.), *Matrilineal Kinship* (Berkeley: University of California Press, 1961. Martin C. Yang in *The Family in the Chinese Revolution* (Cambridge: Harvard University Press, 1961) describes the changes in the clan, and in the relations between family and society, since the Communist Revolution.

William J. Goode, *After Divorce* (Glencoe, Ill.: The Free Press, 1956), and Jessie Bernard, *Remarriage* (New York: Dryden, 1956) analyze the process of family dissolution and reformation.

Most modern works on family change attempt to analyze theoretically the relations between family systems and the larger society, and offer descriptive materials which acquaint us with other societies. Among these are William J. Goode, *World Revolution and Family Patterns* (Glencoe, Ill.: The Free Press, 1963) interpreting the trends in family and social structures over the past half-century in China, Japan, India, sub-Sahara Africa, the Arab countries, and the West; Neil J. Smelser, *Social Change in the Industrial Revolution* (London: Routledge and Kegan Paul, 1951); Ronald P. Dore, *City Life in Japan* (Berkeley: University of California Press, 1958); Marion J. Levy, "Contrasting Factors in the Modernization of China and Japan," in Simon S. Kuznets, Wilbert E. Moore, and Joseph J. Spengler (eds.), *Economic Growth: Brazil, India, Japan* (Durham, N.C.: Duke University Press, 1955); and "Changes in the Family," an issue of the *International Social Science Journal* (1962), 14, devoted to this topic.

118

index

Iberian influence, in New World, 29–30
Illegitimacy (see also Legitimacy): American statistics, 27; as type of family disorganization, 91; effect on children, 25–26; explanations of, 28–30; marriage as solution, 23, 24; rates in various societies, 23–27; social and legal differentiated, 23–24, 27; social controls, 26–27; statistics, 28; types and forms, 22–23
Incest, effects on family, 22, 24
Individual: family-society obligations, 2–5; rebellion against communal living, 5–6; socialization by culture, 10–11, 18–19; socialization by family, 9–10, 67–68
Industrialization: effect on birth rate, 110–111; effect on conjugal family, 84–85; effect on family relations, 1–3, 5, 108–114; upper-class controls over, 109
Instinct: defined, 10; insufficient in man, 11–12
Inter-marriage (see Divorce, inter-faith and inter-racial marriage; Marriage, inter-faith and inter-racial)

Jacobson, P. H., 101
Japan: birth-rate, 3, 112; oyabun-kobun relationship, 65; social organization, 64–65

Kibbutz (Israel), 5, 18
Kindred, 59, 65–66
Kinship: "duo-Iroquois," 104; groupings, 4, 56–66; "normal Dakota," 104; patterns of, 28
Kirkpatrick, Clifford, 72
Kolhoz (Russia), 5, 18
Koller, M. R., 34
Kuznets, S. S., 114

Landis, P. H., 102
Legitimacy (see also Illegitimacy): as basic to family, 20; Malinowski's rule, 21, 28; principle of, 21, 28
Levy, M. J., 114
Lineage: matrilineal, 58–62; omnilineal, 58; patrilineal, 56–58; patrilineal versus matrilineal, 56–58; unilineal, 58, 66
Lobola (see also Bride price), 42
Locke, H. J., 72
Loosley, E. W., 71
Love: as a factor in marriage, 7, 32, 37–43; social controls, 40–41; theory of complementary needs, 38

McClelland, D. C., 77
McGinnis, Robert, 69
Machismo (masculinity), 112–113
Malinowski, Bronislaw, 21, 28, 62
Man, animal traits contrasted, 9, 11–12, 16
Manu, Law of, 2
Marriage: adjustment (happiness) problems, 72 ff.; age statistics, 34; Arab customs, 40–41; caste-hypogamous, 22, 37; child-marriage, 40, 42; endogamous, 33, 35–36; exogamous, 33, 40, 58, 60; heterogamous (inter-racial), 7, 31, 35, 37; Hindu law, 40; homogamous, 33, 36, 81–83; hypergamous, 35; hypogamous, 22, 37; immediate social consequences, 31 ff.; influences in mate choice, 32–33; inter-faith, 95–96; inter-racial (heterogamous), 7, 31, 35, 37; market structure, 32–37; matrilocal, 31; misconceptions about, 3; neolocality, 31, 46, 87, 108; oriental societies, 32, 39; patrilateral (parallel cousin), 40; patrilocal, 31; Polynesian societies, 40–41; religious factors, 35–36; residential propinquity statistics, 34; rules regarding, 22; social-class factors, 33, 35
Marsh, R. M., 86
Marx, Karl, 107
Mating (see also Courtship; Love; Marriage; Sex), 20, 32–33
Matriarchy (see also Matrilineal system), as non-existent, 14
Matrilineal system (see also Descent; Matriarchy), 6, 21, 22
Maturation, 15; defined, 10
Mental disease, effect on family, 7
Merton, R. K., 37, 89, 91, 96

Mobility (see Stratification)
Moore, W. E., 114
Morgan, E. S., 105
Mortality rates, 111, 113–114
Mother-child relationship, 14, 16, 18, 76–78
Mother-daughter relationship, 76–77
Mother-son relationship, 77–78, 106
Motherhood, social responsibility, 21
Murdock, G. P., 46, 66, 70, 92, 104
Murray, H. A., 38

Neolocality, 31; effect on family control, 87; modern, 108; residence rule for households, 46
Nepotism, Chinese attitude, 115
Nisbet, R. A., 89, 91, 96
Nye, F. I., 76

Ogburn, W. F., 107–108
Orphans, modern society, 110

Paleolithic man, 9
Parsons, Talcott, 71
Partrilineage (see Lineage)
Pineo, P. C., 96
Police, role in society, 2
Population explosion, 111
Property: coparcenary (Hindu), 45; related to household type, 44
Puerto Rico: attitude toward children, 112–113; birth-rate statistics, 112; women in, 112–113
Puritans: attitude toward marriage, 114; social control among, 26

Reflexes, defined, 10
Revolutions: bourgeois mobility in, 116; effect on family relations, 2, 85; effect on legitimacy, 23
Rig-Veda, 2
Role relations (see also Family, disorganization), 1, 17–18; American families, 67–68; division of labor, 69–70; kinship, 60; masculine-feminine compared, 69

Schneider, D. M., 60
Seeley, J. R. 71
Separation, as type of family disorganization, 92
Sex (see also Courtship; Love; Marriage; Mating): and family life, 13–14; and social norms, 13; feminine versus masculine attitudes, 71–72; rural morality myth, 27; social and biological differences, 14, 71–72
Sim, R. A., 71
Social change, family systems, 103-113
Social structure, family as, 4–5, 7
Socialization (see also Family; Individual): defined, 10; family survival and, 19
Sociological approach, purposes and methods, 6 ff.
Spengler, J. J., 114
Stephens, W. N., 71
Sterilization (see also Illegitimacy), 113
Stratification: bourgeois mobility, 116. criteria for, 80, 83. family variables related to, enumerated, 81–82. historical data, 82–83. homogamy and mobility, 82–83. sources (evaluation), 83. upper-class families: 82–87; Chinese, 85–86; social controls in, 84–85; stability studies, 86. upward mobility striving, 82–85. weakening of family roles, 86–87

Tiller, P. O., 69

Utopias, 2, 5; Mormons, 2; Oneida community, 2; Plato's Republic, 2, 5; Shaker Community, 2

Vogel, E. W. F., 71

Wallin, P. W., 72
Winch, R. F., 32–33, 34, 38, 69
Women (see also Husband-wife; Marriage; Working mothers): duties of, 1; in modern households, 110; Puerto Rico, 112–113
Working mothers (modern): effect on daughters, 76–77; family results, 75–77

Yanagida, Kunio, 65

Zelditch, Morris, 71

120

index